P9-CRR-197

Paint Your House
With Powdered Milk

AND HUNDREDS MORE OFFBEAT USES FOR BRAND-NAME PRODUCTS

Joey Green

HYPERION

New York

Design by Joey Green

Library of Congress Cataloging-in-Publication Data

Green, Joey.
    Paint your house with powdered milk: and hundreds more offbeat uses for brand-name products / Joey Green. — 1st ed.
        p.   cm.
    Includes bibliographical references and index.
    ISBN 0-7868-8208-5
    1. Home economics.   2. Brand name products—United States.
3. Medicine, Popular.   I. Title
TX158.G679   1996   96–5424
640'.73—dc20   CIP

First Edition
10 9 8 7 6 5 4 3 2 1

Paint Your House
With Powdered Milk

Also by Joey Green

Hellbent on Insanity

The Unofficial Gilligan's Island Handbook

The Get Smart Handbook

The Partridge Family Album

Polish Your Furniture with Panty Hose

Selling Out

Hi Bob!

For Julia

Ingredients

Another Word From Our Sponsor

When I wrote *Polish Your Furniture with Panty Hose*, I had no idea that anyone else on the planet would actually share my enthusiasm for the hundreds of offbeat uses for brand-name products kept secret from the American public. I was convinced I was all alone, a misguided consumer with too much time on his hands, a fluke of the universe.

But with the publication of that book, overzealous Americans from all walks of life came out of the woodwork. I was inundated with hundreds of letters. I suddenly realized that I could turn my love affair with brand-name products into a full-time career, spending the rest of my life investigating the myriad uses for items like Wrigley's Spearmint Gum, Scotch Tape, Miller High Life, and Crayola Crayons. I was ecstatic.

I charged into my new life's mission with all the unbridled enthusiasm of a bargain hunter during a Labor Day White Sale. I unearthed some astonishing truths. Wesson Corn Oil can be used to make bubble bath. Coppertone polishes furniture. Lipton Tea deodorizes feet. Canada Dry Club Soda cleans diamonds. Clorox bleach prolongs the life of cut flowers. But I needed to know more. How did Scotch Tape get its name? Just what is Cream of Tartar? Who invented Tabasco pepper sauce? Are there actually turtles in Turtle Wax? And, more importantly, will anyone besides me really care?

This book is the result of my second sojourn into the heart and soul of American ingenuity. Next time, remind me to bring some Maalox.

Canada Dry

Club Soda

■ **Clean diamonds, rubies, sapphires, and emeralds.** Simply soak the gems in Canada Dry Club Soda.

■ **Make fluffy pancakes, waffles, and matzah balls.** Substitute Canada Dry Club Soda for the liquid used in the recipes.

■ **Make a poor man's lava lamp.** Fill a glass with Canada Dry Club Soda and drop in two raisins. The carbonation will cause the raisins to repeatedly bob to the surface and then sink again.

■ **Clean grease stains from double-knit fabrics.** Pour on Canada Dry Club Soda and scrub gently.

■ **Make inexpensive soft drinks.** Add Canada Dry to fruit juice for a low-cost, healthy beverage.

■ **Remove wine spills or other spots from carpet.** Apply Canada Dry Club Soda to the stain, rub it in, wait a few minutes, then sponge it up.

■ **Clean and shine porcelain fixtures.** Pour Canada Dry Club Soda over the fixtures.

■ **Clean chrome or stainless steel.** Use Canada Dry Club Soda in a spray bottle.

■ **Water your plants.** Feed flat Canada Dry Club Soda to your houseplants or outdoor plants. The minerals in club soda are beneficial to green plants.

■ **Remove food stains from clothes.** Immediately blot up the spills on any washable fabric, sponge with Canada Dry Club Soda, then wash the item in the washing machine through a regular cycle.

■ **Clean countertops.** Pour Canada Dry Club Soda directly on the counter, wipe with a soft cloth, then rinse with warm water and wipe dry.

■ **Relieve an upset stomach.** Drink Canada Dry Club Soda to soothe indigestion.

■ **Clean grease from a car windshield.** Use a spray bottle filled with Canada Dry Club Soda and wipe with paper towels.

■ **Loosen rusty nuts and bolts.** Pour Canada Dry Club Soda over them. The carbonation bubbles away rust.

■ **Change blond hair dyed green by chlorine back to its original color.** Simply rinse your hair with Canada Dry Club Soda.

■ **Preserve newspaper clippings.** Dissolve one Milk of Magnesia tablet in one quart Canada Dry Club Soda. Let the mixture stand overnight. The next day, stir the mixture well, then soak your clipping in the solution for one hour. Blot the newspaper clipping between two sheets of paper towel and place on a screen to dry.

Invented
1930

The Name
Toronto pharmacist J. J. McLaughlin named his first ginger ale McLaughlin's Pale Dry Ginger Ale, later changing the name to Canada Dry Pale Ginger Ale. The word *Canada* denotes the country of the soft drink's origin and the word *dry* suggests nonalcoholic beverages. McLaughlin designed the original Canada Dry trademark—a map of Canada, emblems of the Canadian provinces, and a crouching beaver (the national animal)—inside a shield capped with a crown to symbolize "kinglike quality."

A Short History
In 1904, J. J. McLaughlin, a Toronto pharmacist who had started a small plant that manufactured soda water to be sold to drugstores as a mixer for fruit juices and flavored extracts,

developed a new "dry" ginger ale while trying to improve upon old-style ginger-ale recipes.

Although corner drugstores were the only outlets for distributing carbonated beverages, McLaughlin pioneered techniques for mass bottling that made it possible to serve Canada Dry at baseball games and public beaches.

In 1923, McLaughlin's heirs sold the company for $1 million to P. D. Saylor and J. M. Mathes, who founded the present-day Canada Dry Corporation. In 1930, Canada Dry introduced Tonic Water, Club Soda, Collins Mix, and fountain syrup. In 1986, Cadbury Schweppes, the world's first soft-drink maker, purchased Canada Dry and Sunkist.

Ingredients
Carbonated water, sodium bicarbonate, sodium citrate, potassium sulfate, disodium phosphate

Strange Fact
■ Canada Dry was the first major soft drink company to put soft drinks in cans (1953) and introduce sugar-free drinks (1964).

Distribution
■ Canada Dry also makes Seltzer and Sparkling Water, Vichy Water, Ginger Ale, Collins Mixer, Tonic Water, Sour Mixer, Lemon Sour, Jamaica Cola, Island Lime, Hi-Spot, Half and Half, Concord Grape, Wild Cherry, California Strawberry, Cactus Cooler, Black Cherry Wishniak, Birch Beer, Barrelhead Root Beer, Vanilla Cream Soda, Tahitian

Treat, Sunripe Orange, Peach Soda, and Piña Pineapple.

■ Cadbury Schweppes products are sold in more than 110 countries worldwide.

■ In 1991, Cadbury Schweppes sold over $3.4 million worth of beverages.

■ London-based Cadbury Schweppes uses 800 independent bottlers in the United States, a bottling network second only to the Coca-Cola Company.

For More Information

Canada Dry U.S.A., A division of Cadbury Beverages Inc., Six High Ridge Park, Stamford, CT 06905-0800. Or telephone 1-203-968-5600.

Nonfat Dry Milk

■ **Paint your house.** Mix one and a half cups Carnation Nonfat Dry Milk and one-half cup water until it is the consistency of paint. Blend in a water-based color to make the desired hue. Thin the paint by adding more water; thicken the paint by adding more powdered milk. Brush on as you would any other paint. Let the first coat dry for at least twenty-four hours before adding a second coat. Let the second dry for three days. Early American colonists made their milk paint from the milk used to boil berries, resulting in an attractive gray color. This paint is extremely durable. To strip milk paint, apply ammonia, allow it to dry for about four days, then apply bleach. Make sure you are stripping the paint in a well-ventilated area.

■ **Remove makeup.** Mix a teaspoon of Carnation Nonfat Dry Milk with warm water, apply with a cotton ball, wipe clean, and rinse.

■ **Thaw frozen fish.** Mix one and one-third cups Carnation Nonfat Dry Milk in three and three-quarters cup water. Place the frozen fish in a pan and cover with the milk solution. Milk eliminates the frozen taste, returning the fresh-caught flavor.

■ **Soothe poison ivy, insect bites, and sunburn.** Mix ten ounces Carnation Nonfat Dry Milk and twenty-five ounces water in a quart container. Fill up the container by adding ice cubes and two tablespoons salt. Apply to infected area with a cloth for twenty minutes, three or four times daily.

■ Take a milk bath. Add one-half cup Carnation Nonfat Dry Milk to warm water for a soothing bath.

■ Make a slight crack in a dish or plate disappear. Mix one and one-third cups Carnation Nonfat Dry Milk with three and three-quarters cups water. Place the dish or plate in a pan, cover with the milk solution, then bring to a boil and simmer for forty-five minutes at low heat. In most cases, the crack will vanish.

■ Clean plant leaves. Mix one and one-third cups Carnation Nonfat Dry Milk with seven and three-quarters cups water, and using a soft cloth, wipe the leaves.

■ **Substitute for whipped cream.** Whip one cup Carnation Nonfat Dry Milk in a cup of ice water for five minutes. Use immediately.

■ **Clean silver.** Mix five ounces Carnation Nonfat Dry Milk, twelve ounces water, and one tablespoon Heinz White Vinegar or ReaLemon lemon juice. Let silver stand overnight in the mixture, then rinse clean and dry thoroughly.

Invented
1954

The Name
Legend holds that company founder Elbridge Amos Stuart noticed a box of Carnation cigars in the window of a Seattle shop and decided to use the name for his evaporated milk. The cigars were probably named Carnation to suggest opulence while simultaneously hinting at the word *Corona*.

A Short History
In 1899, Elbridge Amos Stuart founded the Carnation company in Kent, Washington, to manufacture evaporated milk. Purportedly, Stuart had designed a brightly colored label for his cases of evaporated milk before deciding upon a name for his company. Nestlé acquired Carnation in 1985.

Ingredients
Milk, vitamin A, vitamin D_3

Strange Fact

■ Bread factories often add nonfat dry milk to their breads to improve the flavor and enhance the nutritional quality.

■ Nestlé is the world's largest food company.

Distribution

■ Nestlé also makes Carnation Evaporated Milk, Carnation Condensed Milk, Carnation Instant Breakfast drink, and Carnation Breakfast Bars.

■ In the United States, Nestlé's well-known brands include Nestlé, Stouffer's, Hills Bros., Libby's, Carnation, Contadina, Nestea, Nescafé, Taster's Choice, Ortega, and Friskies.

For More Information

Nestlé USA Inc., 800 North Brand Boulevard, Glendale, CA 91203. Or telephone 1-818-549-6000.

Bleach

■ **Extend the life of freshly cut flowers.** Add one-quarter teaspoon (twenty drops) Clorox bleach to each quart of water used in your vase.

■ **Deodorize coolers and thermos bottles.** Wash with diluted Clorox bleach, then rinse.

■ **Remove mold and mildew from outdoor siding, tile, brick, stucco, and patios.** Clean with a mixture of three-quarters cup Clorox bleach per gallon of water.

■ **Remove coffee or tea stains from china cups.** Soak clean china cups for five to ten minutes in a solution of one tablespoon Clorox bleach per gallon of water.

■ **Disinfect garbage cans.** Wash the garbage cans with a solution made from three-quarters cup Clorox bleach to one gallon water. Let stand for five minutes, then rinse clean.

■ **Bail out a boat.** Cap an empty, clean Clorox bleach bottle, cut diagonally across the bottom, and scoop out the water.

■ **Make a scooper.** Cap an empty, clean Clorox bleach bottle, cut diagonally across the bottom, and use it to scoop up flour, sugar, rice, dog food, sand, fertilizer, or snow.

■ **Make a pooper scooper.** Cut an empty, clean Clorox bleach jug in half. Use the half with the handle to scoop.

■ **Clean butcher blocks to prevent bacteria from breeding.** Wash the cutting board with hot, sudsy water and rinse clean. Then apply a solution of three tablespoons Clorox bleach per gallon of water. Keep wet for two minutes, then rinse clean.

■ **Make a hot cap.** Cut off the bottom of an empty, clean Clorox bleach jug and place the jug over the seedlings. Take the cap off during the day, and replace the cap at night. To anchor these hot caps, simply cut off the top of the handle, insert a sharp stick, and drive the stick into the ground.

■ **Remove stains from baby clothes.** Mix one-quarter cup Clorox bleach to one gallon of water in a plastic bucket. Add colorfast clothes and soak for five minutes. Rinse well, then run the clothes through the regular cycle in the washing machine.

■ **Sift soil.** Cut the bottom off an empty, clean Clorox bleach bottle at an angle to make a scooper. Insert a six-inch-diameter piece of one-quarter-inch hardware cloth to rest above the handle hole. Scoop up dirt, sift through the narrow opening, and stones will be caught by the hardware cloth.

■ **Make a fishing or boating buoy.** Cap an empty, clean Clorox bleach jug tightly, tie a rope to the handle, and tie a weight to the other end of the rope. These buoys can also be strung together to mark swimming and boating areas.

■ **Make a carrier for small children's toys and crayons.** Cut a hole in the side of an empty, clean Clorox bleach jug opposite the handle.

■ **Clean mops.** Rinse mops in a bucket of sudsy water and three-quarters cup Clorox bleach per gallon of water.

■ **Clean caulking around bathtubs.** Scrub with a solution of three-quarters cup Clorox bleach to a gallon of water.

■ **Make a clothespin holder.** Cut a hole in the side of an empty, clean Clorox bleach jug opposite the handle, and punch small holes in the bottom for drainage. Hang your new clothespin holder on the clothesline.

■ **Whiten a porcelain sink.** Fill the sink with a solution of three-quarters cup Clorox bleach per gallon of water. Let sit for five minutes.

■ **Make a paint bucket.** Cut a hole in the side of an empty, clean Clorox bleach jug opposite the handle.

■ **Make an anchor.** Fill an empty, clean Clorox bleach bottle with gravel.

■ **Clean a toilet bowl.** Pour in one cup Clorox bleach. Let it stand for ten minutes. Brush and flush.

■ **Clean a rubber sink mat.** Fill the sink with water, add one-quarter cup Clorox bleach, and soak the sink mat for five to ten minutes.

■ **Improvise a funnel.** Cut an empty, clean Clorox bottle in half, remove the cap, and keep it in the trunk of your car as an emergency funnel for motor oil, antifreeze, and water.

■ **Make a bird feeder.** Cut a hole in the side of an empty, clean Clorox bleach jug opposite the handle, and fill with birdseed.

■ **Freshen and disinfect old sponges.** Soak sponges for five to ten minutes in a mixture of three-quarters cup Clorox bleach per gallon of water, then rinse well.

■ **Make a hip bucket for harvesting fruits or berries.** Cut a large hole in the side of an empty, clean Clorox bleach bottle opposite the handle, then string your belt through the handle.

■ **Clean mildew from shower curtains, shower caddies, bath mats, and plastic soap dishes.** Place all the bathroom accessories in the bathtub, fill with two gallons water, and add one and a half cups Clorox bleach. Soak for five to ten minutes, then rinse and drain. The Clorox bleach will have cleaned the bathtub also, so sponge it down too.

■ **Deodorize the garbage disposal in your sink.** Pour one cup Clorox bleach down your drain, then run the hot water for two minutes.

■ **Make dumbbells.** Fill two empty, clean Clorox bleach bottles with sand.

■ **Make a megaphone.** Remove the cap and cut off the bottom of an empty, clean Clorox bleach bottle.

■ **Clean mildew from grout.** Mix three-quarters cup Clorox bleach with one gallon of water, and use an old toothbrush to scrub off the mildew.

■ **Store rock salt for melting snow.** Ice melting products are much easier to dispense from Clorox bleach bottles.

■ **Make glasses sparkle and silverware shine.** Add a capful of Clorox bleach to the dishwasher.

Invented
1916

The Name
Clorox seems to be a combination of the words c*hlorine* and

sodium hydroxide, the two main ingredients used to make sodium hypochlorite bleach.

A Short History

French chemist Claude Louis Berthollet (1748–1822) introduced sodium hypochlorite as an industrial bleach. In 1913, five Oakland investors founded The Electro-Alkaline Company to make industrial-strength bleach using water from salt ponds around San Francisco Bay. The following year the company registered the brand name Clorox and its diamond-shaped trademark. In 1916, the company formulated a less concentrated household bleach, and in 1928, went public. In 1957, Procter & Gamble bought Clorox, resulting in antitrust litigation by the FTC for the next decade. Procter & Gamble was ordered to divest itself of Clorox, and in 1969, Clorox again became an independent company.

Ingredient

5.25 percent solution sodium hypochlorite

Strange Facts

■ According to The Clorox Company, Clorox bleach is an environmentally sound choice because it breaks down naturally after use to little more than salt and water.

■ The shape of the Clorox bottle is a registered trademark of The Clorox Company.

■ Never mix bleach with other household chemicals, such as toilet bowl cleaners, rust removers, acids, or products containing ammonia. To do so will release hazardous gases.

- Never use Clorox on silk or wool; sodium hypochlorite destroys these fibers.
- *Fortune* magazine named Clorox a top ten United States environmental leader in 1993.

Distribution

- Clorox is also available in Fresh Scent, Lemon Fresh, and Floral Fresh.
- Clorox sells its products in ninety-four countries and produces them in more than thirty plants in the United States, Puerto Rico, Canada, Mexico, Argentina, and South Korea.
- Clorox also manufactures Brita water filtering systems, Clorox Clean-Up cleaner, Clorox 2 all-fabric bleach, Combat insect control systems, Formula 409 all-purpose cleaner, Fresh Step cat litter, Hidden Valley Ranch salad dressing, K.C. Masterpiece barbecue sauce, Kingsford charcoal briquets, Kitchen Bouquet browning and seasoning sauce, Liquid-Plumr drain opener, Pine-Sol cleaner, Soft Scrub mild abrasive liquid cleanser, Stain Out soil and stain remover, and Tilex mildew remover.
- In 1995, The Clorox Company's sales topped $1.9 billion.

For More Information

The Clorox Company, 1221 Broadway, Oakland, CA 94612-1888. Or telephone 1-510-271-7000.

Pro Style 1600

■ **Dry salad greens.** Set a Conair Pro Style 1600 on cool, and dry wet leaves of lettuce.

■ **Dry steam off a fogged-up bathroom mirror.** Simply use a Conair Pro Style 1600 to blow hot air at the mirror.

■ **Dry wet boots or sneakers.** Insert the nozzle of a Conair Pro Style 1600 into the boot and use on a low setting for five minutes.

■ **Thaw frozen windows.** Use a Conair Pro Style 1600 to thaw windows that are frozen shut.

■ **Clean crayon marks** from wallpaper. Set a Conair Pro Style 1600 on hot until the wax heats up, then wipe clean with a paper towel.

■ **Do your dusting.** Use a Conair Pro Style 1600 to blow cool air to clean dust off high shelves or out from under appliances, pleated lampshades, carved furniture, crevices, and knickknacks.

■ **Defrost frozen pipes.** Set a Conair Pro Style 1600 on hot and aim at the pipes.

■ **Free a snapshot stuck in a magnetic photo album.** Blow warm air from a Conair Pro Style 1600 underneath the plastic page.

■ **Remove Con-Tact paper.** Set a Conair Pro Style 1600 on warm, work on one section at a time, and gently pull the edges.

■ **Remove candle wax from a table or countertop.** Blow warm air an inch above the drips, then wipe away the wax with a paper towel.

■ **Set cake icing.** Set a Conair Pro Style 1600 on warm and dry cake icing.

■ **Remove a bumper sticker.** Blow it with a Conair Pro Style 1600 set on hot for a few minutes, until the adhesive softens, then peel the bumper sticker off.

■ **Dry the inside of rubber gloves.** Insert the nozzle of a Conair Pro Style 1600 into the glove and blow warm air.

■ **Dry panty hose.** Hang the wet panty hose on the shower rod and blow them dry.

■ **Defrost a jammed automatic ice maker.** Hold a Conair Pro Style 1600 eight inches from the frozen mass of ice cubes until they melt apart.

■ **Remove an adhesive bandage.** Blowing hot air with a Conair Pro Style 1600 at the bandage will soften the adhesive so you can ease off the bandage.

■ **Thaw the frozen lock on a car door.** Before you call the locksmith, use a Conair Pro Style 1600 to thaw the frozen lock.

■ **Remove the wrinkles from plastic tablecloths or shower curtains.** Blow with a Conair Pro Style 1600 set on hot until the plastic softens.

■ **Determine which windows are leaking heat.** Hold a lit candle just inside a window, while someone else goes outside with a Conair Pro Style 1600 and blows air along the frame. If the flame flickers, the window needs caulking.

■ **Dry joint compound.** Use a Conair Pro Style 1600 to speed up the drying process.

■ **Warm cold bed sheets.** Use a Conair Pro Style 1600 to make ice-cold sheets toasty warm.

Invented
1971

The Name

Conair is a conjunction of the words *continental* and *hair*.

A Short History

In 1959, with only $100, Leandro P. Rizzuto and his parents, Julian and Josephine, started Continental Hair Products in New York City to market hair rollers for beauty salons. The company developed the hot comb in 1968 and introduced the first hand-held pistol-grip blow dryer to the United States in 1971. The following year, Continental Hair Products went public at $8.75 per share and, in 1973, acquired Jheri Redding Products, makers of shampoos and conditioners. In May 1976, the company changed its name to Conair Corporation. In 1985, company founder Lee Rizzuto bought the company in the largest leveraged buyout to date by an individual at $300 a share.

Ingredients

Thermoplastic, mica, nickle chrome heater wire, thermal fuse, thermostat, switches, DC motor, rectifier, plastic impeller, screws, heating element

Strange Facts

■ The development of the blow dryer enabled hair salons to accomplish in minutes what used to take hours, thus handling more clients in less time, and thereby increasing revenues.
■ Other products introduced to beauty salons by Conair include curling irons, brushes, shears, shampoos, condition-

ers, beauty soap bars, hair rollers, tipping caps, perms, and perm rods.

Distribution

■ Conair has been the leading designer and manufacturer of professional hair-styling appliances since its founding in 1959.

■ Conair also owns Jheri Redding Products, Cuisinart, Fabergé, and manufactures Southwestern Bell Freedom Phones.

For More Information

Conair Corporation, 150 Milford Road, East Windsor, NJ 08520. Or telephone 1-800-3-CONAIR.

Coppertone

■ **Remove tar spots from car finishes without damaging the finish.** Apply Coppertone to a cloth and rub until the tar glides off.

■ **Prevent skin damage.** Using sunscreen whenever you go out in the sun can prevent wrinkling, discoloration, pronounced blood vessels, and cancerous lesions that may be caused by prolonged exposure to the sun.

■ **Prevent chapped lips.** Coppertone keeps lips moist and healthy.

■ **Moisturize your hands.** The emollients in Coppertone rejuvenate dry skin.

■ **Repel insects.** Slather on Coppertone to keep insects away.

■ **Take a soothing bath.** Add two tablespoons Coppertone to a warm bath as a bath oil.

■ **Soften fingernails.** Warm Coppertone and use as a hot oil treatment to soften nails.

■ **Enjoy a massage.** Coppertone makes an excellent substitute for massage oil.

■ **Relieve itching from insect bites.** Applying Coppertone over the affected areas alleviates itching.

■ **Remove scuff marks from patent leather shoes.** Apply Coppertone to a soft cloth and rub it into the patent leather.

■ **Clean grease and oil from skin.** Rub Coppertone into the skin and wash clean with water.

■ **Polish wood surfaces.** Squeeze Coppertone onto a soft cloth to clean and polish natural wood.

■ **Remove candle wax.** Rub on a dollop of Coppertone to remove candle wax from furniture, carpeting, and clothing.

■ **Clean paint from hands.** Coppertone removes paint and stains from hands more gently than turpentine.

■ **Pry apart two bowls or glasses.** Dribble a few drops of Coppertone down the sides, then slip the bowls or glasses apart.

■ **Clean grease and dirt.** Squeeze Coppertone onto a soft cloth to remove grease stains from Formica surfaces and oven-range hoods.

- **Remove dried glue and gum left by price tags and labels peeled from glass, metals, and most plastics.** Apply Coppertone and wipe clean.

- **Clean ink from hands and vinyl surfaces.** Apply Coppertone and wipe clean.

- **Lubricate pipe joints.** Coppertone works as an oil lubricant for fitting pipe joints together.

Invented
1944

The Name
Coppertone signifies the *copper*-colored skin *tone* sun worshippers strive to obtain.

A Short History
Dr. Benjamin Green, a physician from Miami, Florida, helped the United States military develop sunscreen to protect soldiers stationed in the South Pacific during World War II from getting severe sunburns. After the war, he noticed that tourists in Miami used all kinds of homemade concoctions to bronze in the sun. He began experimenting with different formulas, using his own bald head as a testing ground, until he came up with the recipe for Coppertone suntan cream with the essence of jasmine in 1944. A picture of an Indian chief was on the first bottles, with the slogan "Don't be a Paleface." Little Miss Coppertone replaced him in 1953.

Ingredients

ACTIVE INGREDIENTS: Ethylhexyl p-methoxcinnamate, oxybenzone; INACTIVE INGREDIENTS: Water, sorbitan sesquioleate, sorbitol, glyceryl stearate SE, stearic acid, isopropyl myristrate, triethanolamine, benzyl alcohol, octadecene/MA copolymer, fragrance, dimethicone, carbomer, methylparaben, aloe extract, tocopheryl acetate (Vitamin E acetate), jojoba oil, propylparaben, disodium EDTA

Strange Facts

■ To figure out how many hours of protection you can expect from a sunscreen, take the number of minutes it takes your skin to start burning without sunscreen, multiply by the sun protection factor (SPF) printed on the bottle of Coppertone, and divide the result by sixty. For instance, if you usually burn in thirty minutes, an SPF 8 lotion should protect you for approximately four hours.

■ The higher the SPF of a sunscreen, the higher the price.

■ The higher in the sky the sun is, the higher the SPF number you need. Also, the closer to the equator you are, the stronger the sunscreen you need.

■ Freckles can sometimes be minimized by using sunscreen lotions containing para-aminobenzoic acid (PABA). Freckles are caused by an accumulation of the skin pigment melanin, which responds unevenly to sunlight. Coppertone does not contain PABA.

■ Never use a sunscreen that is more than a year old. Abide by the expiration dates.

■ As a child, actress Jodie Foster appeared in Coppertone commercials.

Distribution

■ Coppertone is the best-selling sunscreen in the United States.

For More Information

Schering-Plough HealthCare Products, Inc. Memphis, TN 38151. Or telephone 1-800-842-4090.

Chalk

■ **Prevent an ant invasion.** Draw a line of Crayola Chalk around windows and doors outside your home, and around water pipes inside your home. Ants will not cross a chalk line.

■ **Clean ring-around-the-collar.** Mark the stain heavily with white Crayola Chalk. The chalk will absorb the sebum oil that holds in the dirt.

■ **Prevent silverware from tarnishing.** Place a piece of Crayola Chalk in your silver chest to absorb moisture.

■ **Cover spots on white suede.** Rub with Crayola Chalk.

■ **Prevent tools from rusting.** Place a few pieces of Crayola Chalk in your toolbox to absorb moisture.

■ **Prevent dampness in a closet.** Tie together a handful of Crayola Chalk and hang the bundle from the clothes rod to absorb moisture.

■ **Prevent a screwdriver from slipping.** Rub Crayola Chalk on the tip.

■ **Polish marble and metal.** Pulverize a few sticks of Crayola Chalk with a mortar and pestle until it is a fine powder. Dip a soft cloth in the powder, wipe the marble or metal, then rinse with clear water, and dry thoroughly.

■ **Fill a hole in a plaster wall.** Insert a piece of Crayola Chalk into the hole, cut it off even with the wall, then plaster.

■ **Repel slugs.** Slugs will not cross a chalk line.

■ **Remove grease.** Rub Crayola Chalk on a grease spot on clothing or table linens, let it absorb the oil, then brush off. Launder as usual.

■ **Draw on sidewalks.** Create games, maps, and adventures.

■ **Prevent costume jewelry from tarnishing.** Place a piece of Crayola Chalk in your jewelry box.

Invented
1902

The Name

Alice Binney, wife of company co-owner Edwin Binney, coined the word Crayola by joining *craie*, from the French word meaning chalk, with *ola*, from *oleaginous*, meaning oily.

A Short History

In 1864, Joseph W. Binney began the Peekskill Chemical Works in Peekskill, New York, producing hardwood charcoal and a black pigment called lampblack. In 1880, he opened a New York office and invited his son, Edwin Binney, and his nephew, C. Harold Smith, to join the company. The cousins renamed the company Binney & Smith and expanded the product line to include shoe polish, printing ink, and black crayons.

In 1900, the company bought a water-powered stone mill along Bushkill Creek near Easton, Pennsylvania, to use slate and other materials from nearby quarries to make slate pencils for schools. The success of the pencils led Binney & Smith to develop chalk for teachers.

Binney & Smith chalk was dustless, made by a process called extrusion, which is still used to this day. Calcium carbonate and water-washed clay are pulverized into powder, mixed together, and then blended with a liquid binder. Balls of dough are then rolled into a cylinder, which is then pressed like toothpaste from a tube. As the long rope of wet chalk emerges, an automatic slicer cuts it into small pieces. The small pieces of chalk are then dried in kilns. For colored chalk, dry powdered pigments are added at the start of the process. Binney & Smith chalk won a Gold Medal for excellence at the 1902 St. Louis Exposition.

Ingredients

Calcium carbonate, water-washed clay, pigments

Strange Facts

■ Chalk—or calcium carbonate—is always 40 percent calcium, 12 percent carbon, and 48 percent oxygen, by weight.

■ Famous chalk deposits include the white cliffs of Dover, England, and the fossil beds in western Kansas.

■ Many chalk deposits were formed during the Cretaceous Period, 136 to 70 million years ago, named from the Latin word for chalk, *creta*.

■ Musician Joni Mitchell released an album entitled *Chalk Mark in a Rainstorm* in 1988.

■ Chalk is used to make rubber goods, paint, putty, polishing powders, and Portland cement.

Distribution

■ Crayola Chalk is available in white, colors, and sidewalk chalk.

For More Information

Crayola Consumer Affairs, P.O. Box 431, Easton, PA 18044-0431. Or telephone 1-800-CRAYOLA.

Crayons

■ **Dye candles.** Melt Crayola Crayons with paraffin to make colored candles.

■ **Rewind a bobbin.** Mark the thread with a contrasting color Crayola Crayon a few yards after starting to wind it onto the bobbin. The crayon mark will alert you when the thread is coming to the end.

■ **Hide scratches on furniture and Formica.** Rub the nick with a matching Crayola Crayon.

■ **Mend a leaking vase.** Hold a match under the pointed end of a Crayola Crayon that matches the color of the vase and let the melted wax drip into the crack. After the wax cools, scrape away the excess.

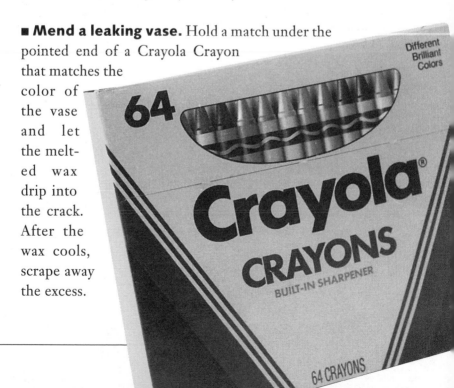

■ **Hide small bleach spots on clothing.** Color the spot with a Crayola Crayon that matches the color of the fabric, then cover with wax paper and iron on a low setting.

■ **Renew the worn dial on a washer or other appliance.** Rub the knob with red or black Crayola Crayon until the indentations of the letters and numbers are filled with colored wax. Then wipe off the excess crayon.

■ **Seal envelopes.** Melt Crayola Crayons as sealing wax for envelopes.

■ **Differentiate hard-boiled eggs from raw eggs in the refrigerator.** Mark the hard-boiled eggs with a Crayola Crayon.

■ **Repair a scratch on an automobile.** Find a matching color Crayola Crayon and work it into the scratch.

Invented
1903

The Name
Alice Binney, wife of company co-owner Edwin Binney, coined the word Crayola by joining *craie*, from the French word meaning chalk, with *ola*, from *oleaginous*, meaning oily.

A Short History
The Peekskill Chemical Works, founded in 1864 by Joseph

W. Binney to manufacture charcoal and black pigment, was renamed Binney & Smith when Binney's son, Edwin, and his nephew, C. Harold Smith, took over the family business. In 1903, the company made the first box of Crayola Crayons, costing a nickel and containing eight colors: red, orange, yellow, green, blue, violet, brown, and black. The now classic box of sixty-four crayons, complete with built-in sharpener, was introduced in 1958. Hallmark Cards, Inc., the world's largest greeting card manufacturer, acquired Binney & Smith in 1984. In 1993, Binney & Smith celebrated Crayola brand's ninetieth birthday by introducing the biggest crayon box ever, with ninety-six colors.

Ingredients

Paraffin wax, stearic acid, colored pigment

Strange Facts

■ In 1949, Binney & Smith introduced another forty colors: Apricot, Bittersweet, Blue Green, Blue Violet, Brick Red, Burnt Sienna, Carnation Pink, Cornflower, Flesh (renamed Peach in 1962, partly as a result of the civil rights movement), Gold, Gray, Green Blue, Green Yellow, Lemon Yellow, Magenta, Mahogany, Maize, Maroon, Melon, Olive Green, Orange Red, Orange Yellow, Orchid, Periwinkle, Pine Green, Prussian Blue (renamed Midnight Blue in 1958 in response to teachers' requests), Red Orange, Red Violet, Salmon, Sea Green, Silver, Spring Green, Tan, Thistle, Turquoise Blue, Violet Blue, Violet Red, White, Yellow Green, and Yellow Orange.

■ In 1958, Binney & Smith added sixteen colors, bringing the total number of colors to sixty-four: Aquamarine, Blue Gray, Burnt Orange, Cadet Blue, Copper, Forest Green, Goldenrod, Indian Red, Lavender, Mulberry, Navy Blue, Plum, Raw Sienna, Raw Umber, Sepia, and Sky Blue.

■ In 1972, Binney & Smith introduced eight fluorescent colors: Atomic Tangerine, Blizzard Blue, Hot Magenta, Laser Lemon, Outrageous Orange, Screamin' Green, Shocking Pink, and Wild Watermelon.

■ In 1990, the company introduced eight more fluorescent colors: Electric Lime, Magic Mint, Purple Pizzazz, Radical Red, Razzle Dazzle Rose, Sunglow, Unmellow Yellow, and Neon Carrot.

■ In 1990, Binney & Smith retired eight traditional colored crayons from its 64-crayon box (Green Blue, Orange Red, Orange Yellow, Violet Blue, Maize, Lemon Yellow, Blue Gray, and Raw Umber) and replaced them with such New Age hues as Cerulean, Vivid Tangerine, Jungle Green, Fuchsia, Dandelion, Teal Blue, Royal Purple, and Wild Strawberry. Retired colors were enshrined in the Crayola Hall of Fame. Protests from groups such as RUMPS (Raw Umber and Maize Preservation Society) and CRAYON (Committee to Reestablish All Your Old Norms) convinced Binney & Smith to release the one million boxes of the Crayola Eight in October 1991.

■ In 1993, Binney & Smith introduced sixteen more colors, all named by consumers: Asparagus, Cerise, Denim, Granny Smith Apple, Macaroni and Cheese, Mauvelous, Pacific Blue, Purple Mountain's Majesty, Razzmatazz, Robin's Egg Blue, Shamrock, Tickle Me Pink, Timber Wolf, Tropical Rain Forest, Tumbleweed, and Wisteria.

■ Washington Irving used the pseudonym Geoffrey Crayon when he published *The Sketch-Book*, a collection of short stories and essays, including "The Legend of Sleepy Hollow" and "Rip Van Winkle."

■ On average, children between the ages of two and seven color for twenty-eight minutes every day.

■ The average child in the United States will wear down 730 crayons by his or her tenth birthday.

■ The scent of Crayola Crayons is among the twenty most recognizable to American adults.

■ The Crayola brand name is recognized by 99 percent of all Americans.

■ Red barns and black tires got their colors thanks in part to two of Binney & Smith's earliest products: red pigment and carbon black. Red and black are also the most popular crayon colors, primarily because children tend to use them for outlining.

■ Binney & Smith is dedicated to environmental responsibility. Crayons that do not meet quality standards are remelted and used to make new crayons. Ninety percent of Crayola products' packaging is made from recycled cardboard. The company also makes sure that the wood in its colored pencils does not originate from tropical rain forests.

Distribution

■ Binney & Smith produces two billion Crayola Crayons a year, which, if placed end to end, would circle the earth four and a half times.

■ Crayola Crayons are also available in Changeables, Glow in the Dark, Glitter, GemTones, Magic Scent, Cosmic Colors, Washable So Big, and Washable Large.

■ Crayola Crayon boxes are printed in eleven languages:

Danish, Dutch, English, Finnish, French, German, Italian, Norwegian, Portuguese, Spanish, and Swedish.

■ Binney & Smith also manufactures Magic Markers, colored pencils, chalk, and Silly Putty.

For More Information

Crayola Consumer Affairs, P.O. Box 431, Easton, PA 18044-0431. Or telephone 1-800-CRAYOLA.

Cream of Tartar

■ **Clean ring-around-the-collar.** Wet the collar with warm or hot water, rub in Cream of Tartar, then launder as usual.

■ **Repel ants.** Sprinkle Cream of Tartar around entrances to ant nests and into cracks and crevices.

■ **Clean a bathtub.** Make a paste from Cream of Tartar and hydrogen peroxide, scrub with a brush, and rinse thoroughly.

■ **Cook with a buttermilk substitute.** Mix one cup milk with one and three-quarters tablespoons Cream of Tartar for use as a buttermilk substitute in recipes.

■ **Clean the blackened inside of an aluminum pot.** Boil a solution of two teaspoons Cream of Tartar and one quart water in the pot for several minutes.

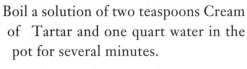

■ **Remove rust stains from washable fabrics.** Make a paste of Cream of Tartar and hot water, rub into the stain, let sit for ten minutes, then launder as usual.

■ **Clean porcelain.** Sprinkle Cream of Tartar on a damp cloth and rub the porcelain surface.

■ **Make tartrate baking powder.** Blend together one-half teaspoon Cream of Tartar, one-quarter teaspoon Arm & Hammer Baking Soda, and one-quarter teaspoon Kingsford's Corn Starch.

Invented
1903

The Name
Cream signifies the refining process used to procure the *tartar* that adheres to the inside of wine barrels.

A Short History
In 1889, McCormick & Company was started in Baltimore in one room and a cellar by twenty-five-year-old Willoughby M. McCormick and his staff of two girls and a boy. The company's first products were root beer, flavoring extracts, and fruit syrups and juices—all sold door-to-door. The company entered the spice field in 1896 when McCormick bought F. G. Emmett Spice Company of Philadelphia and had all the spice machinery shipped to Baltimore. In 1947, the McCormick Company acquired A. Schilling & Company of San Francisco, a coffee, spice, and extract house, gaining coast-to-coast distribution with the slogan "United to serve the nation's good taste."

Ingredient

Potassium bitartrate

Strange Facts

■ Cream of Tartar is derived from argol, the crude tartar sediment deposited on the sides of casks during wine-making.

■ Cream of Tartar is also called potassium bitartrate and has the chemical formula $KHC_4H_4O_6$.

■ Cream of Tartar is also used to manufacture baking soda, to tin plate metals, and as a laxative in medicines.

■ Cream of Tartar has an indefinite shelf life if kept tightly closed and stored away from heat.

■ McCormick/Schilling obtains its supply of Cream of Tartar from Italy, where short people crawl through the very small holes in open wine casks to scrape out the residue left after the wine has been fermented and drained out.

Distribution

■ McCormick products are distributed under the Schilling label in the western United States.

■ McCormick & Company, Inc., is the largest spice company in the world, with annual sales of $1.7 billion.

For More Information

McCormick & Company, Inc., P.O. Box 208, Hunt Valley, MD 21030-0208.

Food Coloring

■ **Tint wallpaper paste.** Add a few drops food coloring to wallpaper paste so you can see how well you are covering the wallpaper.

■ **Make your own gift-wrapping paper.** Add five drops food coloring to one cup water, making one cup for each one of the four colors. Stack several sheets of white tissue paper on top of each other, fold them in half, in half again, and in half again. Dip each one of the four corners into a different color solution without soaking the paper. Let the tissue dry on newspaper, unfold, then iron flat.

■ **Make colorful macaroni jewelry for kids.** Add a few drops food coloring to a bowl of water. Dip dry macaroni noodles in the water, drain, and dry. Then make necklaces by stringing the colored macaroni noodles together.

■ **Paint snow.** Put a teaspoon of food coloring in a spray bottle filled with water and let kids spray designs on snow.

■ **Make fried chicken golden brown.** Add a few drops of yellow food coloring to vegetable oil before frying. The chicken will absorb the food coloring and become a golden brown.

■ **Color the water in a fish tank.** Adding a few drops of food coloring will make a colorful environment without harming the fish.

■ **Differentiate hard-boiled eggs from raw eggs in the refrigerator.** Before hard-boiling eggs, add food coloring to the water to tint them.

■ **Recolor small bleach spots on clothing.** Mix food coloring with water to make the proper shade and apply to the spot.

■ **Make fingerpaint.** Mix two cups soap flakes, two cups liquid laundry starch, and five drops food coloring in a large bowl. Blend with a wire whisk until the mixture has the consistency of whipped cream. Or mix one-quarter cup Kingsford's Corn Starch with two cups cold water, boil until thick, pour into small containers, and color with food coloring.

■ **Tint flowers.** Mix food coloring in warm water and place the flower stems in the solution overnight. The stems will absorb the colors by morning, revealing intriguing designs in different colors.

■ **Make clown makeup.** Mix two tablespoons Kingsford's Corn Starch, one tablespoon solid shortening, and several drops food coloring.

■ **Make colorful glues.** Fill an empty SueBee honey bear with Elmer's Glue-All and tint with a few drops of food coloring.

Invented
1890

The Name
Food coloring obviously refers to an edible dye used to color food.

A Short History
Spices and condiments were probably used as colors as long ago as 1000 B.C. In all likelihood, colorants taken from natural minerals, plants, and animals were developed along with spices. In the eighteenth and nineteenth centuries, unscrupulous food manufacturers used colorings to disguise spoiled foods. In 1856, Sir William Henry Perkins discovered the first synthetic dye, derived from coal tar.

In the United States, the Federal Pure Food and Drug Act of 1906 attempted to regulate food dyes. The Federal Food, Drug and Cosmetic (FD&C) Act of 1938 made certification mandatory for any synthetic food color. Synthetic food colors, previously known by their common names, were numbered to avoid confusion with inedible dyes. Three categories were created for designated color names: FD&C, D&C, and External D&C. The 1960 Color Additives Amendment gave the Food and Drug Administration (FDA) the authority to set safe limits for the amount of colors permitted in foods, drugs, and cosmetics. The FDA also required all food coloring to undergo premarketing safety clearances.

There are three types of food coloring: natural dyes (anthocyanins, betanins, carotenoids, and chlorophylls), nature identical dyes (synthetic counterparts of colors and pigments derived from natural sources), and synthetic dyes— FD&C dyes (water soluble compounds) and FD&C lakes (aluminum hydrate extensions). As of 1986, FDA regulations permit only nine FD&C dyes and seven FD&C lakes in our food supply.

Ingredients

Water, propylene glycol, FD&C yellow No. 5, FD&C red No. 40, FD&C blue No. 1, FD&C red No. 3, 0.1 percent propylparaben (preservative), and sulfiting agents (contained in blue and green colors only)

Strange Facts

■ The ancient Aztecs used cochineal, a red dye prepared from the dried bodies of female *Dactylopius coccus*, an insect that lives on cactus plants in Central and South America. Cochineal is still used today in food coloring, medicinal products, cosmetics, inks, and artists' pigments.

■ In the United States, the first federal regulation concerning food colors was an 1886 act of Congress allowing butter to be colored.

Color Blending Chart	FOR ICINGS & BAKED GOODS	FOR COLORED EGGS
	Gently squeeze sides of bottle, adding color drop by drop to obtain desired shade.	To one-half cup boiling water add one teaspoon vinegar and twenty drops desired color. For other colors, refer to chart. Dip hard-boiled eggs until desired shade is obtained. After color dries, it will not rub off.
COLORS	**NUMBER OF DROPS REQUIRED**	
Orange	1 red, 2 yellow	6 red, 14 yellow
Chartreuse	12 yellow, 1 green	24 yellow, 2 green
Peach	1 red, 3 yellow	—
Turquoise	5 blue, 1 green	15 blue, 5 green
Purple	1 red, 1 blue	10 red, 4 blue
Rose	5 red, 1 blue	15 red, 5 blue

■ Studies show that people judge the quality of food by its color. In fact, the color of a food actually affects a person's perception of its taste, smell, and feel. Researchers have concluded that color even affects a person's ability to identify flavor.

Distribution

■ McCormick products are distributed under the Schilling label in the western United States.

■ An extensive survey conducted by the National Academy of Sciences in 1977 estimated that the average American consumes 327.6 milligrams of FD&C color additives every day. That's sixteen times the Recommended Daily Allowance for iron. According to the survey, every day each American consumes an average of 100 milligrams of FD&C Red Dye No. 40, 43 milligrams of FD&C Yellow Dye No. 5, and 37 milligrams FD&C Yellow Dye No. 6.

For More Information

McCormick & Company, Inc., P.O. Box 208, Hunt Valley, MD 21030-0208.

Trash Bags

■ **Sled down a snow-covered hill.** Tie a GLAD Trash Bag around your bottom like a diaper, and slide down the hill.

■ **Improvise a raincoat.** Cut slits in a GLAD Trash Bag for head and arms.

■ **Cover your barbecue.** Protect your outdoor grill by covering it with a GLAD Trash Bag.

■ **Make a solar-powered camping shower.** Fill a GLAD Trash Bag with water, tie it to a solid tree branch, and let the sun heat the water. After you lather up with soap, poke a small hole in the bag to rinse off.

■ **Protect chandeliers and hanging lamps when painting a ceiling.** Pull a GLAD Trash Bag up over the lighting fixture and tie it up as high on the chain as possible.

■ **Travel with a plastic laundry bag.** Pack a GLAD Trash Bag in your suitcase.

■ **Prevent ice from accumulating on a car windshield.** Cut open a GLAD Trash Bag, place it over the entire windshield, and close the car doors over the edges of the bag to hold it in place. When you're ready to go, brush off any snow and peel off the plastic bag.

■ **Make a Hawaiian grass skirt.** Cut off the bottom of a GLAD Trash Bag and cut long strips one inch wide to within three inches of the pull cord.

■ **Make waterproof stuffing for outdoor cushions, bathtub toys, and stuffed animals.** Cut a GLAD Trash Bag into strips and use it as the stuffing.

■ **Make dust covers for clothes.** Cut a small hole in the center of the bottom of a GLAD Trash Bag and slip the bag over the top of a suit or a dress on a hanger.

■ **Make a ground cloth for camping trips.** Place your sleeping bag on top of several GLAD Trash Bags to keep out moisture.

■ **Hold bath toys.** Punch holes in a GLAD Trash Bag and hang it on the shower nozzle to hold bath toys.

■ **Improvise a plastic sheet.** Cut a GLAD Trash Bag down the sides and place it under the sheets.

■ **Make streamers.** Cut a GLAD Trash Bag into strips, starting from the open end and stopping two inches before you reach the bottom.

■ **Waterproof a backpack.** Cover the backpack with a GLAD Trash Bag and cut small slits in the bag for the straps of the backpack.

■ **Collect aluminum cans for recycling.** Hang a GLAD Trash Bag on the inside of a kitchen cabinet or pantry door.

■ **Make a shop apron.** Cut open the bottom of a GLAD Trash Bag, put it over your head, and slip your arms through the handles.

■ **Improvise a windbreaker.** Cut holes in a GLAD Trash Bag for your head and arms and wear it under your coat.

■ **Store your winter clothes.** Fill a GLAD Trash Bag with your sweaters, add a few mothballs, and seal with a twist tie.

■ **Make a scarecrow.** Cut a GLAD Trash Bag into long strips, staple to the lip of a Dixie Cup, and then nail the cup to a tree or a pole in your garden. The plastic strips blowing in the wind will scare birds away.

Invented
Early 1960s

The Name

GLAD apparently signifies the pleasure and joy consumers will experience when their trash is clad in these pleasingly convenient garbage bags.

A Short History

In 1917, National Carbon Company, makers of carbons for streetlights and owner of the Eveready trademark, merged with Union Carbide, manufacturers of calcium carbide— along with Linde Air Products (oxygen), Prest-O-Lite (calcium carbide), and Electro Metallurgical (metals)—to form Union Carbide & Carbon Corporation. In 1920, the company established its own chemicals division, which developed ethylene glycol (antifreeze), eventually marketed as Prestone. In 1957 the company changed its name to Union Carbide Corporation and in the early 1960s introduced GLAD plastic household products. In 1985, Union Carbide sold its line of GLAD garbage bags to First Brands Corporation.

Ingredient

Polyethylene

Strange Facts

■ The Man from GLAD, seen in television commercials during the 1970s, was a take-off on *The Man from U.N.C.L.E.*
■ In 1984, a tank at Union Carbide's pesticide plant in Bhopal, India, leaked five tons of poisonous methyl isocyanate gas, killing more than 3,000 people and permanently

injuring 50,000 people. It was the world's worst industrial accident in recorded history, resulting in a $470 million settlement in India's Supreme Court in 1989.

Distribution

■ GLAD Handle-Tie Garbage Bags are available in Tall Kitchen Garbage Bags, Regular Trash Size, Large Trash Size, Clear Large Trash Size, and Clear Kitchen Size.

For More Information

First Brands Corporation, P.O. Box 1999, Danbury, CT 06813-1999. Or telephone 1-203-731-2300.

Gold Medal

Flour

■ **Make Play Dough.** Add fifty drops food coloring to two cups water. Then add two cups Gold Medal flour, one cup salt, one teaspoon Cream of Tartar, and two tablespoons Wesson Corn Oil. Mix well. Cook and stir over medium heat for three minutes (or until the mixture holds together). Turn onto a board or a cookie sheet and knead to the proper consistency. Store in an airtight container.

■ **Make glue.** Mix Gold Medal flour and water to a pancake-batter consistency for use on paper, lightweight fabric, and cardboard.

■ **Make papier-mâché.** In a medium-size bowl mix one cup Gold Medal flour with two-thirds cup water to a thick-glue consistency. To thicken,

add more flour. Cut newspaper strips approximately one to two inches in width. Dip each strip into the paste, gently pull it between your fingers to remove excess paste, and apply it to any empty bottle, carton, canister, or disposable container. Repeat until the surface is completely covered. Let dry, then decorate with poster paint. After the paint dries, coat with shellac.

■ **Clean white kid gloves.** Rub Gold Medal flour into the leather, then brush clean.

■ **Clean brass and copper.** Mix equal parts Gold Medal flour and Morton Salt and add one teaspoon Heinz White Vinegar to make a paste. Spread a thick layer on the brass and let dry. Wash off paste and rinse clean.

■ **Clean a deck of playing cards.** Place the deck of cards in a paper bag, add four tablespoons Gold Medal flour, and shake briskly. Remove the cards from the bag and wipe clean.

■ **Repel ants.** Fill cracks and make a line with Gold Medal flour where ants enter. Ants will not cross through flour.

Invented
1880

The Name
Gold Medal flour is cleverly named after the gold medal this flour won at an 1880 exhibition.

A Short History

In 1866, Cadwallader Washburn founded the Washburn Crosby Company. After winning a gold medal for flour at an 1880 exhibition, the company introduced the Gold Medal flour trademark. In 1921, the advertising department of Washburn Crosby created a fictional spokeswoman, Betty Crocker (named in honor of a retired company director, William G. Crocker) so that correspondence to housewives could go out with a woman's signature. In 1924, the company introduced Wheaties ready-to-eat cereal. Four years later, James F. Bell, president of Washburn Crosby, consolidated the company with other mills around the country (including Red Star, Rocky Mountain Elevator, Kalispell Flour, and Sperry Flour Company) to form General Mills, the world's largest miller.

Ingredients

Wheat flour, malted barley flour, niacin (a B vitamin), iron, thiamin mononitrate (vitamin B_1), and riboflavin (vitamin B_2)

Strange Facts

■ General Mills introduced Bisquick in the 1930s and Cheerios in 1941, which, along with flour, generated enough sales to allow the company to pay dividends throughout the 1930s and 1940s.

■ During the European Renaissance, when the medieval ideal of feminine beauty required a woman's skin to be as white as a lily and her cheeks as red as a rose, peasants, unable to afford expensive cosmetics, made do with wheat flour and beet juice.

■ Since 1972, most of the flour found in home kitchens has been used for baking cookies.

■ Betty Crocker's first formal portrait was drafted by artist Neysa McMein in 1936. Betty is now in her eighth incarnation.

■ In the 1940s, Eleanor Roosevelt was voted the most well-known woman in America, followed by Betty Crocker.

Distribution

■ General Mills is the second largest cereal manufacturer in the United States.

■ Gold Medal flour is available in All-Purpose flour, Whole Wheat flour, Better for Bread bread flour, Better for Bread Wheat Blend flour, Better for Biscuits self-rising flour, Wondra quick-mixing flour, and Softasilk cake flour.

■ Besides Gold Medal flour, General Mills also makes Betty Crocker dessert mixes, Cheerios, Cocoa Puffs, Golden Grahams, Kix, Lucky Charms, Raisin Nut Bran, Total, Trix, Wheaties, Bisquick, Bugles, Fruit Roll-Ups, Hamburger Helper, Nature Valley Granola Bars, Pop Secret Microwave Popcorn, Potato Buds Instant Mashed Potatoes, and Yoplait Yogurt.

For More Information

General Mills, Inc., P.O. Box 1113, Minneapolis, MN 55440. Or telephone 1-800-328-6787.

Kingsford's

Corn Starch

■ **Kill cockroaches.** Mix equal parts Kingsford's Corn Starch and plaster of Paris. Sprinkle the mixture in cracks and crevices. Cockroaches will eat the mixture and "petrify."

■ **Cure athlete's foot.** Sprinkle Kingsford's Corn Starch on your feet and in your shoes to absorb moisture and reduce friction.

■ **Relieve bad sunburn pain.** Add enough water to Kingsford's Corn Starch to make a paste, and apply directly to the burn.

■ **Clean a carpet.** Sprinkle Kingsford's Corn Starch on the carpet, wait thirty minutes, then vacuum clean.

■ **Clean bloodstains.** Immediately cover the spot with a paste of Kingsford's Corn Starch and cold water. Rub gently, place the object in the sun until dry to draw the blood into the corn starch, then brush off. Repeat if necessary.

■ **Make spray starch for clothing.** Mix one tablespoon Kingsford's Corn Starch and one pint cold water. Stir to dissolve the corn starch completely. Fill a spray bottle and use as you would any starch. Be sure to shake vigorously before each use.

■ **Substitute for baby powder and talcum powder.** Apply Kingsford's Corn Starch sparingly when diapering a baby. Corn starch is actually more absorbent than talcum powder, but apply lightly since it does cake more readily.

■ **Help rubber gloves slip on easily.** Sprinkle Kingsford's Corn Starch inside the gloves.

■ **Shine your car.** When buffing your car, sprinkle a tablespoon of Kingsford's Corn Starch on the wipe rag to remove excess polish easily.

■ **Shampoo your hair.** Kingsford's Corn Starch can be used as a dry shampoo. Work into your hair, then brush out.

■ **Prevent or kill mildew in damp books.** Sprinkle Kingsford's Corn Starch throughout the book to absorb the moisture from damp pages, wait several hours, then brush clean. If the pages are mildewed, brush the corn starch off outdoors to keep mildew spores outside the house.

■ **Detangle knots.** Sprinkle a stubborn knot with a little Kingsford's Corn Starch.

■ **Make fingerpaints.** Mix one-quarter cup Kingsford's Corn Starch with two cups cold water, boil until thick, pour into small containers, and color with food coloring.

■ **Absorb excess polish from furniture.** After polishing furniture, sprinkle on a little Kingsford's Corn Starch and rub wood with a soft cloth.

■ **Clean silver.** Make a paste with Kingsford's Corn Starch and water. Apply with a damp cloth, let dry, then rub off with cheesecloth.

■ **Remove grease or oil stains from smooth fabric.** Apply Kingsford's Corn Starch to the spot, wait twelve hours, brush off, then launder as usual.

■ **Make white clown makeup.** Mix two tablespoons Kingsford's Corn Starch with one tablespoon solid shortening. To tint it, add food coloring.

■ **Give your dog a dry shampoo.** Rub Kingsford's Corn Starch into your dog's fur, then comb and brush out.

■ **Clean stuffed animals.** Rub Kingsford's Corn Starch into the toy, let stand for five minutes, then brush off.

■ **Prevent pastry dough from sticking to the cutting board and rolling pin.** Sprinkle the cutting board and rolling pin with Kingsford's Corn Starch—it's tasteless—before rolling out the dough.

■ **Clean a deck of playing cards.** Place the deck of cards in a paper bag, adding four tablespoons Kingsford's Corn Starch, and shake briskly. Remove the cards from the bag and wipe clean.

■ **Soothe skin irritations.** Apply a paste made of equal parts Kingsford's Corn Starch, zinc oxide, and castor oil.

■ **Thicken gravy.** Corn starch has twice the thickening power of flour. When a gravy, sauce, soup, or stew recipe calls for flour, use half as much corn starch to thicken. One tablespoon of corn starch equals two tablespoons flour.

■ **Relieve the pain and discomfort caused by hemorrhoids.** Ben Charles Harris, author of *Kitchen Medicines*, suggests mixing one tablespoon Kingsford's Corn Starch in enough water to make a paste, gradually adding more water to measure a pint, boiling the mixture for a few minutes, allowing it to cool, and then using it in an enema.

Invented
1842

The Name
Kingsford's Corn Starch was named after company founder Thomas Kingsford. Corn starch itself is named for the starch found in corn.

A Short History
All green plants manufacture starch through photosynthesis

to serve as a metabolic reserve, but it wasn't until 1842 that Thomas Kingsford developed a technique for separating starch from corn. The corn-refining industry emerged fifty years later. In 1894, twenty corn starch and syrup producers grouped together as National Starch Manufacturing to prevent severe price competition and establish quotas, gaining 70 percent of the corn starch market, until their association disintegrated. By 1906, price wars forced New York Glucose to merge with Glucose Sugar Refining Company, forming Corn Products Refining Company (CPRC), the first stable corn-refining company, controlling 64 percent of the starch and 100 percent of the glucose output in the United States.

Over the years, CPRC faced a series of antitrust suits, forcing the company to sell portions of its business and eliminate "phantom freight" charges. By 1954, CPRC had only a 46 percent share of corn-grinding capacity, producing several brands, including Mazola, Karo, ARGO, and Kingsford's. In 1958, the corn refinery merged with Best Foods—producers of Hellmann's, Best Foods, Skippy, and Rit brands—and bought C. H. Knorr soups. In 1969, the company was renamed CPC International and, since 1988, acquired over fifty companies.

Ingredients

100 percent pure corn starch

Strange Facts

■ Corn starch, the most important starch manufactured in the United States, can be hydrolyzed for the manufacture of D-glucose and corn syrup.

■ Approximately one-third of the corn starch produced in America is sold for food purposes.

Distribution

■ CPC operates twenty-nine plants in the United States, eight in Canada, thirty-eight in Europe, fourteen in Africa and the Middle East, thirty-four in Latin America, and eleven in Asia.

■ In 1993, CPC International sold more than $1.1 billion worth of refined corn products worldwide.

■ CPC International also makes Hellmann's mayonnaise, Best Foods, Mazola, Knorr soups, Skippy peanut butter, and Thomas' English Muffins.

For More Information

Best Foods, CPC International, Inc., International Plaza, P.O. Box 8000, Englewood Cliffs, NJ 07632-9976. Or telephone 1-800-344-2746.

Tea Bags

■ **Deodorize your feet.** Boil three or four Lipton Flo-Thru Tea Bags in one quart of water for ten minutes. Add enough cold water to make a comfortable soak. Soak your feet for twenty to thirty minutes, then dry and apply foot powder. Do this twice a day until the odor is under control. Then continue twice a week to keep it under control. Tannin, which can be found in tea, is a drying agent.

■ **Dye graying white fabrics.** If Clorox bleach won't whiten a graying white garment, soak the item in hot, strong-brewed Lipton tea until it is a shade darker than you desire. Then rinse in cold water and let dry.

■ **Highlight brown hair.** Rinse red or brown hair with brewed Lipton tea for golden highlights.

■ **Relieve sunburn pain.** Pat your sunburn with wet Lipton Flo-Thru Tea Bags.

■ **Accelerate the germination of grass seeds.** Mix two tablespoons cold, strong-brewed Lipton tea into each pound of seed, cover, and set in the refrigerator for five days. Before sowing, spread the seed to dry for a day or two on newspapers on the garage or basement floor.

■ **Deodorize stuffy rooms.** Mix one quart brewed Lipton tea and four tablespoons ReaLemon lemon juice, strain through a Mr. Coffee filter, and store in empty spray bottles.

■ **Soothe a sore throat or laryngitis.** Drink brewed Lipton tea with ReaLemon lemon juice or SueBee Honey.

■ **Invigorate houseplants.** Water ferns and other houseplants once a week with a tepid, weak-brewed Lipton tea.

■ **Polish black lacquer.** Wash black lacquer pieces with strong-brewed Lipton tea, then wipe dry with a soft cloth.

■ **Help relieve diarrhea.** Drink plenty of Lipton tea and eat toast. The tannin in tea is reported to be helpful in cases of diarrhea, while its liquid replaces fluids lost by the body.

■ **Soothe tired eyes.** Place Lipton Flo-Thru Tea Bags soaked in cool or lukewarm water over your eyes for at least fifteen minutes.

■ **Soothe a burn.** Apply wet Lipton Flo-Thru Tea Bags directly to the burn, or secure in place with gauze.

■ **Stop gums from bleeding after having a tooth pulled.** With your finger, press a cool, moist Lipton Flo-Thru Tea Bag against the cavity.

■ **Fix a broken fingernail.** Cut a piece of gauze paper from a Lipton Flo-Thru Tea Bag to fit the nail, coat with Maybelline Crystal Clear nail polish, and press gently against the break. Then cover with colored nail polish.

■ **Clean varnished woodwork.** Cold Lipton tea is a good cleaning agent for any kind of woodwork.

■ **Tenderize meat.** Add equal parts strong-brewed Lipton tea and double-strength beef stock to a tough pot roast or stew. The tannin in tea is a natural meat tenderizer.

Invented
1890

The Name
Lipton tea is named after the founder of the company, Sir Thomas Lipton.

A Short History
Born in 1850 in Glasgow, Scotland, Sir Thomas Lipton sold cured meats, eggs, butter, and cheeses from a small store that grew into a chain of stores throughout Scotland and England. In 1888, Lipton entered the tea trade, and two years later entered the American market, pioneering packaged tea

with the famous Flo-Thru bag. He was knighted in 1898 and made a baronet in 1902. A yachting enthusiast, Lipton made five unsuccessful attempts to win the Americas cup. His portrait, complete with nautical attire, adorns all Lipton tea packages. He died at the age of 81 in 1931.

Ingredients

Orange pekoe and pekoe cut black tea

Strange Facts

■ According to an ancient Chinese legend, the first cup of tea was brewed by Emperor Shennong in 2737 B.C. when a few leaves from a tea plant accidentally fell into water he was boiling.

■ Since tea plants grow more slowly in cooler air, yielding a better-flavored leaf, the best teas are grown at altitudes between 3,000 and 7,000 feet. Tea connoisseurs consider the tea grown on the slopes of the Himalayan mountains near Darjeeling, India, to be among the world's finest.

■ Although tea is often considered a British custom steeped in tradition, tea was not introduced to England (or the American colonies) until British merchants formed the East India Company in 1600.

■ During the Boston Tea Party on December 16, 1773, American colonists, disguised as Indians and protesting British taxes on imported tea, boarded three ships in Boston harbor and dumped into the water 342 chests of tea valued at 9,000 British pounds, an event that led to the Revolutionary War.

Distribution

■ Lipton calls itself the "brisk" tea because it contains a blend of approximately twenty quality teas selected from around the world. Teas are chosen to provide the proper taste, color, and consistency.

■ Tea is the most popular beverage in the world, and Lipton tea is the best-selling tea in America.

■ According to the United States Department of Agriculture, in 1991, the average American consumed 2.8 gallons of tea, 6.5 gallons of coffee, 7.3 gallons of juice, 25.7 gallons of milk, and 43.2 gallons of soft drinks.

■ India produces one third of the world's tea, followed by China and Sri Lanka.

■ Lipton also makes Decaffeinated Tea, Lemon Flavor Tea, and Tropical Flavor Tea.

For More Information

Thomas J. Lipton Company, 800 Sylvan Avenue, Englewood Cliffs, NJ 07632. Or telephone 1-800-697-7887.

Lubriderm

■ **Shine shoes.** Rub a dab of Lubriderm on each shoe and buff thoroughly.

■ **Shave.** If you run out of shaving cream, slather on Lubriderm.

■ **Soothe a sunburn.** After soaking or using compresses, smooth on some bath oil. Then moisturize with Lubriderm.

■ **Remove a ring stuck on a finger.** Apply Lubriderm around the ring band and slide the ring off.

■ **Slip on rubber gloves.** Apply Lubriderm before putting on rubber gloves. The heat from washing dishes will also help the moisturizing skin cream melt in.

■ **Prevent hang-nails.** Moisturize your cuticles daily.

Rub Lubriderm into the flesh surrounding your nails to keep the area soft.

■ **Prevent dry skin in an air-conditioned or steam-heated room.** Use extra Lubriderm. Air-conditioning and steam heat dry skin.

■ **Eliminate static cling.** Rub a dab of Lubriderm into your hands until it disappears, then rub your palms over your panty hose or slip.

Invented
1946

The Name
Lubriderm is apparently a clever combination of the words *lubricate* and the suffix *-derm*, derived from the Greek word *derma*, meaning skin.

A Short History
Texas Pharmacal developed Lubriderm Lotion in 1946 for dermatologists as a base for their own formulations of topical drugs to treat dermatological conditions involving dry skin. Lubriderm quickly gained a reputation as the dermatologist's choice as a compounding base, and demand for the moisturizer escalated. In the 1950s, Warner-Lambert bought Texas Pharmacal, and the product is now marketed by the Warner-Wellcome Consumer Health Care Group.

Ingredients

Water, mineral oil, petrolatum, sorbitol, lanolin, stearic acid, lanolin alcohol, cetyl alcohol, tri (PPG-3 myristyl ether) citrate, triethanolamine, methylparaben, methyl-dibromo glutaronitrile/phenoxyethanol, fragrance, ethyl-paraben, propylparaben, butylparaben, sodium chloride

Strange Facts

■ Original Lubriderm Lotion, created for dermatologists, penetrates dry skin with pure moisturizing emollients to restore the skin's naturally healthy look and feel. The oil in Lubriderm Lotion is quickly absorbed into the dry upper layer of the skin, leaving it feeling clean and fresh.

■ Lubriderm contains only one ingredient derived from animals. Lanolin, an occlusive agent found in Lubriderm, is derived from the wool of sheep. The sheep are shaved, and the lanolin is taken from the wool.

■ Lubriderm is an oil-in-water emulsion. Since oil and water don't mix, Lubriderm Lotion is formulated with an emulsifier that holds the oil within the water. Oil in water allows dry skin to take up water better than water in oil. With water on the outside of the emulsion, some of this water evaporates, and the skin is cooled. The oil on the inside of the emulsion breaks down and forms a protective barrier over the skin surface, keeping the remaining supplemental water and the available natural moisture in the skin to provide moisturization.

■ Clinical studies have shown that after continued use, the moisturizing benefits of Lubriderm Lotion last for days.

Distribution

■ Warner-Lambert has operations in more than 130 countries.

■ Lubriderm Dry Skin Care Lotion is available in Original Fragrance and Fragrance Free. Lubriderm is also available in Seriously Sensitive Lotion, Moisture Recovery Gel Creme, and Alpha Hydroxy Lotion and Creme.

For More Information

Warner-Lambert Company, 201 Tabor Road, Morris Plains, NJ 07950-2693. Or telephone 1-800-223-0182.

MasterCard

■ **Scrape frost from a windshield.** If nothing else is available, use an old MasterCard to master the possibilities.

■ **Open a locked door.** Slide an old MasterCard between the door and the frame to press the latch into the door. If the bevel faces the other way, cut the card into an L shape, insert it, and pull it toward you.

■ **Scrape candle wax from a tabletop.** Use an old MasterCard to remove as much wax as possible. Then place a sheet of paper towel over the wax and press gently with a warm iron to absorb the remaining wax.

■ **Clean your fingernails.** The corner of a MasterCard works as a manicure tool.

■ **Scrape paint.** Use an old MasterCard to scrape off peeling paint.

■ **Play guitar.** If you lose a guitar pick, use a corner of an old MasterCard.

Invented
1966

The Name

MasterCard was originally called MasterCharge. The word *master* implies predominance, while the word *charge* means to purchase on credit. The words *master* and *card* suggest the predominant credit card.

A Short History

Shopkeepers often let regular customers charge items to their account to be paid monthly, eventually letting them pay for large purchases in monthly installments. In the 1930s, oil companies offered motorists "courtesy cards" to use service stations across the country, and department stores began offering customers "revolving credit." In 1950, tarpaulin salesman Francis Xavier McNamara founded Diners Club, the first multipurpose credit card offered by an intermediary between the vendor and the buyer, popularized by an article in *The New Yorker*'s "Talk of the Town."

The Franklin National Bank in New York offered the first bank credit card in 1951. Numerous credit cards issued by independent banks quickly followed, but, by the mid-1960s, MasterCharge and BankAmericard (renamed MasterCard and Visa in the 1970s) dominated the field. Both MasterCard and Visa are credit associations that sign up banks that then offer cards to consumers.

Ingredients

Plastic, ink, magnetic strip, holographic image (color foil and ultraviolet ink)

Strange Facts

■ An average of 200 million credit cards are used every day in the United States.

■ Americans charged a total of $480 billion on credit cards in 1990. That's equal to $1 million every minute.

■ The typical American credit card holder carries nine credit cards and owes over $2,000.

■ In 1983, MasterCard became the first credit card company to introduce the laser hologram on its cards to combat counterfeiting.

■ In 1988, MasterCard became the first payment card issued in the People's Republic of China.

■ In 1990, Citibank, the largest issuer of credit cards in America, made over $610 million in profits on its Visa and MasterCard operations, according to Spencer Nilson, editor of *The Nilson Report*, an industry newsletter.

■ According to *Consumer Reports*, 80 percent of all purchasing in the United States is done on credit.

■ The magnetic strip on a MasterCard holds two or three tracks of information. The first track contains your name, expiration date, card type, and data such as your PIN and credit limit. The second track holds your account number, start date, and discretionary data. The third track holds information for ATM use.

■ The first six digits of your account number indicate the company that issued the card. The second four digits identify region and branch information. The last five digits are your account number (the last digit being a check number for security purposes).

Distribution

■ As of 1994, there were 238.9 million MasterCards in circulation worldwide. Of those, 135.6 million were held by Americans.

■ MasterCard is accepted in more than 12.7 million locations in more than 220 countries and territories around the world.

For More Information

MasterCard International Incorporated, 888 Seventh Avenue, New York, NY 10106. Or telephone 1-212-649-4600.

Maxwell House

Coffee

■ **Dye fabric brown inexpensively.** Soak the fabric in a bucket of strong, black, Maxwell House Coffee. This technique is also a good way to cover up an unremovable coffee stain on a white tablecloth.

■ **Fertilize a garden or houseplants.** Work Maxwell House Coffee grounds into the topsoil.

■ **Repair scratched woodwork.** Mix one teaspoon instant Maxwell House Coffee with two teaspoons water. Apply to the scratch with a cotton ball.

■ **Start a charcoal fire.** Remove the top and bottom of an empty Maxwell House Coffee can and punch a few holes in the sides of the can. Stand the can in your barbecue grill, fill it with Kingsford charcoal briquets, add lighter fluid, and light. When the coals glow, remove the hot can with tongs and set in a safe place.

■ **Prevent dampness in closets.** Fill an empty Maxwell House Coffee can with Kingsford charcoal briquets, punch holes in the plastic cover, and set on the floor in the back of the closet.

■ **Repel ants.** Sprinkle dried Maxwell House Coffee grounds outside doors and cracks. Coffee deters ants.

■ **Relieve a hangover.** Drink a couple of cups of Maxwell House Coffee. Coffee acts as a vasoconstrictor, reducing the swelling of blood vessels, the cause of headache.

■ **Spread grass seed or fertilizer.** Punch holes in the bottom of an empty can of Maxwell House Coffee, fill with grass seed or fertilizer, cover with the plastic lid, and shake the can as you walk through your garden.

■ **Transport live fishing bait.** Keep worms in a Maxwell House Coffee can filled with moist coffee grounds.

■ **Keep toilet paper waterproof while camping.** Carry a roll of toilet paper inside an empty Maxwell House Coffee can.

■ **Protect baby tomato plants.** Remove the tops and bottoms from Maxwell House Coffee cans, place a can over each plant, and step on the can to set it firmly in the soil. Remove cans when plants are a few weeks old.

■ **Grow better melons.** Raise melons off the ground by resting them on top of upside-down empty Maxwell House Coffee cans pushed into the soil. The metal cans accumulate heat, making the fruit ripen earlier while also repelling insects.

■ **Keep paintbrush bristles from bending while soaking in solvent.** Put solvent in an empty Maxwell House Coffee can, cut an X in the plastic lid, and push the brush handle up through the slit so that the brush hangs in the can rather than resting on its bristles.

■ **Highlight brown or red hair.** Rinse your hair with Maxwell House Coffee for a rich and shiny color.

■ **Deodorize the refrigerator and freezer.** Place a bowl filled with Maxwell House Coffee grounds on the back shelf.

■ **Patch woodwork.** Mix dry instant Maxwell House Coffee with spackling paste until you achieve the desired brown tone, fill the crack or hole, and smooth with a damp cloth.

■ **Clean a restaurant grill.** Pour leftover brewed Maxwell House Coffee over a warm or cold grill and wipe clean.

■ **Wrap cookies and candies.** Cover an empty Maxwell House Coffee can with wrapping paper, fill with cookies or candy, cover with the plastic lid, then wrap.

■ **Cover spots on black suede.** Sponge on a little black Maxwell House Coffee.

■ **Make emergency lights.** Wrap reflector tape around a couple of empty Maxwell House Coffee cans and store in the trunk of your car for emergencies.

■ **Make stilts.** String rope through holes punched in the closed ends of two empty Maxwell House Coffee cans.

■ **Store nails, screws, bolts, and washers.** Maxwell House Coffee cans make perfect storage containers.

■ **Improvise a gelatin mold.** Use an empty Maxwell House Coffee can.

■ **Store cat box litter in the trunk of your car for emergencies.** Cat box litter, stored in empty Maxwell House Coffee cans, can be used for traction under the wheels of a car stuck in snow or ice.

■ **Flavor spaghetti.** Add one-quarter to one-half teaspoon instant Maxwell House Coffee to spaghetti sauce. Coffee gives store-bought spaghetti sauce brown coloring and a less acidic flavor.

Invented
1892

The Name
Maxwell House Coffee is named after the Maxwell House hotel in Nashville, Tennessee.

A Short History

In 1873, Joel Owsley Cheek, a 21-year-old farm boy, left his home in Burkesville, Kentucky, to seek his fortune in Nashville. After a short stint as a traveling salesman for a wholesale grocery firm, he set up his own grocery firm and began experimenting to originate his ideal coffee blend, which he began selling in 1882. Among his clients was one of America's top-ranked hotels, the Maxwell House of Nashville. The elite hotel guests raved over the new "Maxwell House Coffee." In 1892, Cheek named his blend Maxwell House Coffee.

Legend has it that Theodore Roosevelt tasted the coffee while a guest at the Hermitage, Andrew Jackson's old Nashville home. When asked if he wanted another cup, Roosevelt purportedly responded, "Will I have another? Delighted! It's good to the last drop!" thus giving birth to the catchy slogan and the logo depicting a tilted coffee cup dripping one last drop.

In 1928, C. W. Post's cereal company acquired Cheek-Neal Company, changed the name to Maxwell House Products Company, and, the following year, acquired Clarence Birdseye's General Foods Company. Postum changed its name to General Foods Corporation, and, in 1985, was acquired by Philip Morris Companies, Inc. Three years later, Philip Morris Companies, Inc., acquried Kraft, Inc., and, in 1989, combined it with General Foods Corporation to form Kraft General Foods, Inc. In 1995, Kraft General Foods, Inc., shortened its name to Kraft Foods, Inc.

Ingredient

100 percent pure coffee

Strange Facts

■ Maxwell House Coffee's slogan, "Good to the Last Drop," ignited a controversy over the proper use of the word *to*. Pundits asked, "What's wrong with the last drop?" A renowned English professor at Columbia University finally decreed that the word *to* is good usage and includes the last drop. The word *until* would preclude the last drop. The slogan was first used by Coca-Cola in 1908.

■ Coffee, native to Ethiopia and cultivated and brewed in Arab countries for centuries, was not introduced into Europe until the seventeenth century.

■ The average coffee tree, grown from seed, bears its first fruit after five to eight years and yields approximately one pound of coffee beans each year.

■ While the coffee plant has many varieties, two species, *Coffea arabica* and *Coffea robusta*, provide 99 percent of the world's coffee.

■ Americans now drink an average of 1.75 cups of coffee a day, nearly half of what they drank in 1962.

Distribution

■ Maxwell House Coffee is also available in Maxwell House Lite, Maxwell House Master Blend, Maxwell House Filter Packs, Maxwell House Filter Pack Singles, and Maxwell House Filter Packs Decaffeinated.

For More Information

Kraft General Foods, Inc., P.O. Box 131, White Plains, NY 10625. Or telephone 1-800-432-6333.

Miller High Life

■ **Kill slugs.** Fill jar lids with half an inch of Miller High Life. Slugs love beer and drown in it.

■ **Shampoo your hair.** Miller High Life is a terrific shampoo for oily hair, although shampooing your hair too frequently with beer can eventually dry out your scalp and lead to dandruff.

■ **Marinate meats.** Marinating inexpensive cuts of meat in Miller High Life for approximately an hour before cooking increases the flavor and tenderness.

■ **Lure insects away from an outdoor party or barbecue.** Place open cans of Miller High Life around the perimeter of the yard. Stinging insects, like wasps and yellow jackets, will be attracted to the beer instead of your guests.

■ **Fertilize a lawn.** Jerry Baker, author of *The Impatient Gardener*, suggests mixing one cup Listerine, one cup Epsom salts, one cup liquid soap, and one cup ammonia in a one-quart jar, and then filling the rest of the jar with beer. Spray this on up to 2,500 square feet of lawn with a hose-attached sprayer in May and again in late June.

■ **Set your hair.** Miller High Life works as a setting lotion. Shampoo your hair, towel dry, and then spray beer onto your hair, using a pump bottle before setting. It's excellent for oily hair.

■ **Cook with Miller High Life.** Will Anderson, author of *From Beer to Eternity*, offers recipes for Beer Soup (requiring one quart beer), a Beer Sandwich (calling for three-quarters cup beer), and a Beer Omelet (made with one-half cup beer). The Miller Brewing Company offers a free recipe book, including recipes for Pot Roast with Beer (calling for one cup beer), Beer Burgers (needing three-quarters cup beer), and Beer Cookies (requiring one cup beer).

■ **Bake bread.** Sprinkle three to five tablespoons sugar over three cups self-rising flour, add one can Miller High Life, and knead. Put the dough in a greased loaf pan, let stand for five minutes, then bake for forty-five minutes at 350°F. Rub butter over the top and bake for an additional five minutes. Serve warm.

Invented

1855

The Name

Miller beer was named after the company founder Frederick Miller. In 1903, when Miller's son, Carl, sought a new name for the light-colored pilsner, his wife's uncle, Ernst Miller, chanced upon a building down in New Orleans called High Life Cigars. The Miller Brewing Company paid $25,000 for the factory and the right to use the name. The word beer is believed to come from the Celtic word *beor*, used to describe the malt brew produced in the monasteries of North Gaul. In 1906, the company adopted "The Champagne of Bottled Beer" slogan to describe Miller High Life.

A Short History

No one knows exactly when people started brewing beer, but the earliest record of beer can be found on a Mesopotamian tablet (circa 7000 B.C.) inscribed with a cuneiform recipe for the "wine of the grain." Anthropologists believe Mesopotamians and Egyptians first developed the process of malting (making barley more suitable for brewing by germinating the barley grains, developing the enzymes that transform starch into fermentable sugars). Vikings brewed *bior* in Scandinavia, and Julius Caesar found the various tribes of the British isles drinking ale when he and his Roman legions landed. More than likely, Gaulish monks first used hops, which have a preservative and aromatic effect on beer.

After revolutionary upheavals ravaged Europe in 1848, hundreds of thousands of Germans immigrated to America, bringing with them a love of golden lager beer and the knowledge of how to brew it. A young German immigrant, Frederick Miller, formerly the brew master at Hohenzollern

Castle in Germany, bought the small, five-year-old Plank Road Brewery west of Milwaukee in 1855. Miller produced 300 barrels of high-quality lager beer in his first year, storing the brew in a network of caverns in the hillside behind the brewery.

By Miller's death in 1888, the brewery was producing 80,000 barrels of beer annually. By 1954, under the leadership of Frederick C. Miller, the founder's grandson, Miller Brewing Company was the ninth largest brewery in the world, shipping two million barrels each year. When Philip Morris, the worldwide tobacco and consumer-packaged goods company, acquired the company in 1970, Miller was the nation's seventh largest brewer, producing 5.1 million barrels of beer that year. Philip Morris marketed Miller High Life with the popular "Miller Time" advertising campaign, and by the 1990s, Miller was brewing more than 40 million barrels per year, making it the second largest brewery in the United States, after Anheuser-Busch.

Ingredients
Malted barley, select cereal grains, pure water, choicest hops

Strange Facts
■ During the Inca empire in Cuzco, Peru, beer made from maize was a luxury served by the state on ceremonial occasions.

■ The Pilgrims landed at Plymouth Rock in December 1620, because, in the words of a diarist aboard the *Mayflower*, "We could not now take time for further search or consideration, our victuals being much spent, especially our beere."

■ George Washington, Thomas Jefferson, and William Penn brewed beer on their estates.

■ Miller Brewing, founded twenty-one years before the first Budweiser was brewed in 1876, is the world's third largest beer producer (after Anheuser-Busch and Heineken).

■ In 1855, Frederick Miller established a beautifully landscaped twenty-acre beer garden in Milwaukee that attracted weekend crowds for bowling, dancing, fine lunches, and old fashioned *gemutlichkeit*. The garden caught fire on July 4, 1891, and was ultimately torn down in 1909.

■ In 1850, Frederick Charles Best and his brother dug tunnels in the hills behind the Plank Road Brewery to store beer in the days before refrigeration. When Frederick Miller bought the brewery five years later, he expanded the tunnels to a total of 600 feet—enough to store 12,000 barrels of beer. With the advent of refrigeration, the brewery abandoned the caves until 1952, when a portion of the caves were opened to tourists through the Miller Caves Museum.

■ When company president Carl Miller took his adolescent daughter Loretta on a visit to the brewery, he sat her at the end of the bar in the dining room. Loretta held her hand up dramatically, inadvertently providing Miller with the inspiration for the High Life "Girl in the Moon." Carl's brother, Fred, sketched the High Life girl, using a photograph of Loretta. Between 1907 and 1911, the "Girl in the Moon" graced metal beer-serving trays used in beer gardens, hotels, bars, and restaurants. The trays and other "Girl in the Moon" promotional materials are now collector's items.

■ Hollywood actor Arthur Franz portrayed Miller Brewing Company founder Frederick Miller in a 48-minute commercial film, *With This Ring*, produced in 1955. The movie, filmed in Hollywood, Milwaukee, and Sigmaringen, Germany, followed the story of a fictitious "brewer's ring" allegedly passed on from generation to generation over the 100-year history of the Miller Brewing Company.

■ In 1983, Miller received the National Environmental Industry Award from the President's Council on Environmental Quality for excellence in air and water pollution control.

■ As a founding member of Keep America Beautiful, the Miller Brewing Company has reduced the amount of aluminum in its cans by 45 percent, saving 100 million pounds of aluminum a year. In addition, recycled materials make up approximately 80 percent of its aluminum cans. Packing materials are reused three to four times before they are sent to be recycled—keeping 750,000 pounds of corrugated cardboard out of the waste stream and reducing the company's need for new corrugated cardboard by 75 percent.

■ Beer is 92 percent water.

Distribution

■ In 1994, the Miller Brewing Company sold over $4 billion worth of beer.

■ Miller also makes Löwenbräu, Meister Bräu, Milwaukee's Best, Molson, Red Dog, and Sharp's.

■ Miller operates breweries in Milwaukee, Wisconsin; Eden, North Carolina; Albany, Georgia; Fort Worth, Texas; Trenton, Ohio; and Irwindale, California.

■ Beer is the most popular alcoholic beverage in America, consumed regularly by more than 80 million Americans.

■ Beer accounts for nearly 87 percent of all alcoholic beverages consumed in the United States. The average American drinks approximately 23 gallons of beer every year.

■ According to New York's Simmons Market Research Bureau, 55.1 percent of all beer drinkers surveyed in 1985 were college educated, while 38.9 percent of all beer drinkers were high school dropouts.

For More Information

Miller Brewing Company, 3939 West Highland Boulevard, P.O. Box 482, Milwaukee, WI 53201-0482. Or telephone 1-800-MILLER6.

No Stick Cooking Spray

■ **Speed up a sled.** Spray Pam No Stick Cooking Spray on the bottom of a sled or an inner tube before taking it out in the snow.

■ **Dry nail polish.** After polishing your nails, spray with Pam No Stick Cooking Spray.

■ **Prevent cut grass from sticking to the blades of a lawn mower.** Spray the cutting blade of the lawnmower with Pam No Stick Cooking Spray before cutting the lawn.

■ **Lubricate bicycle chains and roller-skate wheels.** Spray with Pam No Stick Cooking Spray.

■ **Prevent tomato sauce stains on plastic containers.** Spray the insides of the containers with Pam No Stick Cooking Spray before filling the containers with any food containing tomatoes.

■ **Season a cast-iron pot or skillet.** Wash in warm, soapy water after each use, wipe thoroughly dry, coat the inside with Pam No Stick Cooking Spray, then wipe clean with a sheet of paper towel.

■ **Make salt stick to air-popped popcorn.** Spray the popcorn with Pam No Stick Cooking Spray, then salt it.

■ **Help snow or dirt slide off a shovel.** Spray Pam No Stick Cooking Spray on the snow or garden shovel.

■ **Prevent a key from sticking in the lock.** Spray the lock and/or the key with Pam No Stick Cooking Spray.

■ **Clean soap scum from a shower door.** Spray Pam No Stick Cooking Spray on a soft cloth, and wipe clean.

■ **Make cleaning a grater less grating.** Before using the grater, spray it with Pam No Stick Cooking Spray to make cleanup easier.

■ **Make defrosting the freezer easier.** After defrosting the freezer, spray it with Pam No Stick Cooking Spray.

■ **Prevent dishwasher runners from sticking.** Spray the runners with Pam No Stick Cooking Spray.

■ **Prevent squeaky door hinges.** Spray with Pam No Stick Cooking Spray.

■ **Make cleaning the broiler pan easier.** Spray the pan with Pam No Stick Cooking Spray before cooking.

■ **Prevent Saran Wrap from sticking to a pie or cake.**
Spray the underside of the plastic wrap with Pam No Stick
Cooking Spray.

■ **Make cleaning artificial snow from windows easier.**
Before decorating windows with artificial snow, spray the
glass lightly with Pam No Stick Cooking Spray.

■ **Prevent waffles from sticking to a waffle iron.**
Spray Pam No Stick Cooking Spray on the waffle iron.

■ **Prevent dough from sticking to a table.** Spray the
surface with Pam No Stick Cooking Spray.

■ **Prevent car doors from freezing shut.** Spray the
rubber gaskets with Pam No Stick Cooking Spray. The
vegetable oil seals out water without harming the gasket.

Invented

1957

The Name

Pam is believed to be named after the daughter of company
cofounder Arthur Meyerhoff. Coincidentally, the archaic
meaning of the word *pamper* is "to indulge with rich food."

A Short History

In 1959, Arthur Meyerhoff and Leon Rubin started Pam
Products, Inc., in Chicago, but business wasn't too success-

ful. Two years later, Rubin received a patent for a nonstick cooking oil consisting of lecithin dissolved in an organic solvent and dispensed from an aerosol container. Meyerhoff and Rubin founded Gibraltar Industries to market this new Pam cooking spray, introducing the product on local Chicago television cooking shows. Sales began taking off after Carmelita Pope, a well-known Chicago personality, endorsed Pam and demonstrated its many uses.

In 1971, Gibraltar Industries merged with American Home Products, makers of Chef Boyardee foods and a leader in women's health care products. American Home Products acquired the patent for Pam and began marketing the product through its Boyle-Midway Division, which introduced Butter Flavor Pam in 1984 and Olive Oil Pam in 1989. The following year, American Home Products assumed responsibility for the Pam cooking spray business.

Ingredients

Canola oil, grain alcohol from corn (added for clarity), lecithin from soybeans (prevents sticking), and propellant

Strange Facts

■ A 1.25 second spritz of Pam No Stick Cooking Spray compares to a tablespoon of butter, margarine, or canola oil. A tablespoon of butter contains 11.5 grams of fat, a tablespoon of margarine contains 11 grams of fat, a tablespoon of canola oil contains 14 grams of fat, a 1.25 second spritz of Pam No Stick Cooking Spray contains only 1 gram of fat.

■ Pam No Stick Cooking Spray, the original and number-one-selling aerosol nonstick cooking spray in the United

States, is all natural and does not contain any sodium or cholesterol.

■ American Home Products replaced the fluorocarbons in Pam No Stick Cooking Spray with other edible oils to meet environmental standards.

Distribution

■ American Home Products sold $152 million worth of food products in 1993.

■ American Home Products makes the estrogen drug Premarin, the most prescribed drug in America, and the contraceptive implant Norplant. The company also makes Advil, Anacin, Chap Stick, Chef Boyardee, Crunch 'n Munch, Denorex, Gulden's, Jiffy Pop, Preparation H, and Robitussin.

For More Information

American Home Food Products, Inc., Five Giralda Farms, Madison, NJ 07940. Or telephone 1-800-PAM-4YOU.

Cut-Rite Wax Paper

■ **Make hangers glide along a clothes rod.** Rub a sheet of Reynolds Cut-Rite Wax Paper over the clothes rod and hangers will glide back and forth more easily.

■ **Preserve autumn leaves.** Place the leaves between two sheets of Reynolds Cut-Rite Wax Paper, then place the wax paper between two sheets of brown paper. Press with a warm iron to seal, then trim the paper around the leaves.

■ **Prevent shoe polish from smearing.** Let the shoe polish dry, then rub with a sheet of Reynolds Cut-Rite Wax Paper to remove the excess polish. Use a second sheet of Cut-Rite Wax Paper as a work surface to prevent the shoe polish from spattering the floor.

■ **Prevent a mess when whipping cream with an electric beater.** Cut two small holes in the middle of a sheet of Reynolds Cut-Rite Wax Paper, slip the stem of the beaters through the holes, and attach to the machine. Lower the beaters into the mixing bowl, keeping the wax paper over the bowl, and turn on the machine.

■ **Save stamps.** Keep stamps between sheets of Reynolds Cut-Rite Wax Paper to prevent them from sticking together.

■ **Prevent spatters in the microwave.** Cover spaghetti

and meatballs, chili, or other saucy foods with Reynolds Cut-Rite Wax Paper.

■ **Make a crayon sun-catcher.** Using a small pencil sharpener, shave crayons onto a sheet of Cut-Rite Wax paper. Fold the wax paper in half, covering all the shavings. Press with a warm iron until the crayon shavings melt. When cool, thread string through the top of the wax paper and hang in a window.

■ **Improvise a diaper changing pad.** A sheet of Cut-Rite Wax Paper can be used as an easy-to-tote changing mat.

■ **Save ingredients when measuring.** When measuring flour, sugar, baking mix, or other dry ingredients, crease a sheet of Cut-Rite paper down the middle, open it up, and place it on the kitchen countertop. Spoon the ingredient into a dry measuring cup, level it off with a knife or spatula, letting the excess fall on the wax paper. Pick up the wax paper, and pour the excess back in its canister.

■ **Never grease a cake pan again.** Place each pan on a sheet of Cut Rite Wax Paper, trace around the bottom of the pan, cut out the wax paper circle, and place it in the pan. After baking and cooling, loosen the sides of the cake with a knife.

Invert the cake onto a cooling rack, remove the pan, and peel off the wax paper for a smooth surface that's ready to frost.

■ Store candles. Roll candles in a sheet of Cut-Rite Wax Paper before placing them in a drawer or storage box to protect them from getting scuffed.

■ Resurface a metal sliding board. Rub a sheet of Reynolds Cut-Rite Wax Paper on the metal slide.

■ Prevent a skin from forming in paint cans. Place the paint can lid on a sheet of Reynolds Cut-Rite Wax Paper, trace around the lid, and cut a pattern from the wax paper. Lay the wax paper directly on the surface of the paint in the can and replace the lid. The wax paper will keep oil- or water-based paints fresh for months.

■ Shine kitchen appliances and counters. Buff appliance exteriors and counter tops with a sheet of Reynolds Cut-Rite Wax Paper.

■ Fix a stuck metal zipper. To make a metal zipper work smoothly, run a sheet of Reynolds Cut-Rite Wax Paper up and down the teeth.

▣ Seal a wooden salad bowl. Wash and dry the wooden salad bowl thoroughly, then rub the entire bowl with a sheet of Reynolds Cut-Rite Wax Paper.

■ Clean and shine a floor between waxings. Put a piece of Reynolds Cut-Rite Wax Paper under the mop head and clean.

Invented

1927

The Name

Reynolds Metals was named after company founder Richard S. Reynolds Sr. The Reynolds logo, used since 1935, was inspired by Raphael's version of *St. George and the Dragon*. The legend of England's patron saint, depicted in several noted paintings, symbolizes the crusading spirit.

A Short History

Early in his career, Richard S. Reynolds worked for his uncle, tobacco king R. J. Reynolds. In 1919, the young Reynolds started his own business, the U.S. Foil Co., supplying tin-lead wrappers to cigarette and candy companies. When the price of aluminum dropped in the 1920s, Reynolds switched to the new lightweight, noncorrosive metal. In 1924, U.S. Foil bought the company that made Eskimo Pies, the ice cream product wrapped in foil. Four years later, Reynolds purchased Robertshaw Thermostat, Fulton Sylphon, and part of Beechnut Foil, adding the companies to U.S. Foil to form Reynolds Metals. Foreseeing a need for aluminum if the United States became involved in World War II, Reynolds Metals began mining bauxite (aluminum ore) in Arkansas in 1940 and opened its first aluminum plant near Sheffield, Alabama, the following year. Reynolds Metals pioneered the development of aluminum siding in 1945 and Reynolds Wrap Aluminum Foil in 1947. In 1982, the company introduced Reynolds Plastic Wrap.

Ingredients

Paper and wax

Strange Fact

■ Each year Reynolds Metals sells enough Cut-Rite Wax Paper to circle the globe more than fifteen times.

Distribution

■ Reynolds Metals also makes Reynolds Wrap Aluminum Foil, Reynolds Plastic Wrap, Reynolds Oven Bags, and Reynolds Freezer Paper.

■ Reynolds Metals is the second largest aluminum company in the United States (behind Alcoa), and the third largest aluminum company in the world (behind Canada's Alcan Aluminum).

For More Information

Reynolds Metals Company, 6601 West Broad Street, P.O. Box 27003, Richmond, VA 23261-7003. Or telephone 1-804-281-2000.

Transparent Tape

■ **Trim bangs.** Place a piece of Scotch Transparent Tape across the bangs and cut the hair just above the tape.

■ **Help keep long-stemmed flowers standing upright in a vase.** Crisscross Scotch Transparent Tape across the mouth of the vase.

■ **Avoid losing small parts when fixing an appliance.** Before dismantling the item, tape a strip of Scotch Transparent Tape, adhesive side up, on your worktable. Place the parts on the tape in the order you remove them, so they are ready to be reassembled.

■ **Make sewing snaps on clothing a snap.** Tape the snaps, hooks, and eyes to the garment, sew them on right along with the Scotch Transparent Tape, then pull the tape off.

■ **Fix a broken eyeglass lens temporarily.** Use a small piece of Scotch Transparent Tape at the top and bottom of the crack.

■ **Restring a necklace of beads of graduated sizes.** Tape a strip of Scotch Transparent Tape, adhesive side up, on a desktop. Arrange beads in order on the tape, then restring.

■ **Attach a sewing pattern to fabric.** Use Scotch Transparent Tape to tape the pattern to the material, then cut the pattern, leaving a reinforced edge.

■ **Prevent a plaster wall from crumbling when driving a nail into it.** Make a small X over the spot with two strips of Scotch Transparent Tape, then drive in the nail.

■ **Caddie nails.** Place nails between layers of Scotch Transparent Tape so they are readily available.

■ **Prevent knickknacks from scratching highly polished table tops.** Line the bottoms of the objects with Scotch Transparent Tape.

■ **Fix a frayed shoelace tip.** Wrap the frayed end with a small strip of Scotch Transparent Tape.

■ **Protect labels on prescription medicines.** Cover the label with Scotch Transparent Tape.

■ **Stop a run in panty hose.** In an emergency, place a piece of Scotch Transparent Tape over the snag.

■ **Prevent small children from poking objects into electrical outlets.** Cover the sockets with Scotch Transparent Tape.

■ **Save recipes clipped from magazines.** Simply use Scotch Transparent Tape to attach the clipped recipes to index cards.

■ **Keep seed markers in the garden legible.** Cover the seed markers with Scotch Transparent Tape.

■ **Sew in a zipper.** Baste the seam closed, press open, tape the zipper face down along the basted seam on the wrong side of the fabric (allowing the tape to hold the zipper flat). Sew on a machine, then remove the tape and basting.

■ **Straighten bent stems in your garden.** Make a splint with a Popsicle stick and Scotch Transparent Tape.

■ **Kill ants.** Wrap a long strip of Scotch Transparent Tape around your hand, adhesive side out, to pick up an advancing line of ants.

Invented

1929

The Name

The name Scotch tape resulted from an ethnic slur foisted upon manufacturers of the tape—although the product does not have any connection with Scotland or the Scottish.

In 1925, the automobile industry, eager to satisfy Americans' craving for two-tone cars, had difficulty making a clean, sharp edge where one color met another. Richard Drew, a 25-year-old laboratory employee at the Minnesota Mining and Manufacturing Company (better known as 3M), developed a two-inch-wide strip of paper tape coated with a rubber-based adhesive. To cut costs, the masking tape was coated with a strip of glue one-quarter-inch only wide along the edges, instead of covering the entire two-inch width.

Unfortunately, the tape failed to hold properly, and the painters purportedly told the 3M salesmen to "Take this tape back to those Scotch bosses of yours and tell them to put adhesive all over the tape, not just on the edges." The 3M Company complied, but when the salesman returned to the automobile paint shop, a painter derogatorily asked him if he was still selling that "Scotch" tape, launching a trade name based on an ethnic slur denoting stinginess. The name, like the improved tape, stuck.

A Short History

In 1929, the Flaxlinum Company of St. Paul asked 3M to develop a moisture-proof, transparent tape to seal the wrapping on insulation slabs in railroad refrigerator cars. Richard Drew, the inventor of masking tape, coated Du Pont's new moisture-proof cellophane with a pressure-sensitive rubber-based adhesive, which, while not strong enough for insulation slabs, was marketed as Scotch Cellulose Tape to the trade in 1930 as "the only natural, transparent, quick seal for 'Cellophane.'"

In the meantime, the process for heat-sealing cellophane had been developed, virtually eliminating the need for Scotch tape. But Americans, caught in the midst of the Depression, soon discovered that Scotch tape could be used to mend torn pages of books, fix broken toys, and seal open cans of evaporated milk.

Because the end of Scotch tape tends to stick to the roll, camouflaged by its transparency, in 1932 John A. Borden, a 3M sales manager, invented the tape dispenser with a ledge to keep the end of the tape away from the roll and incorporated a serrated edge to cut the tape.

Ingredients
Cellophane, adhesive

Strange Facts
■ After cows ate the resin-coated fabric on the rudder section of a 1946 Taylor craft airplane, the plane's owner, Edward Bridwell, used Scotch Transparent Tape to repair it.

■ Ornithologists have used Scotch Transparent Tape to cover cracks in the soft shells of fertilized pigeon eggs, allowing the eggs to hatch.

■ Landlords in Bangkok, Thailand, have used Scotch Transparent Tape to repair cracks in the walls of tenants' apartments.

■ During the Depression, banks first used Scotch Transparent Tape to mend torn currency.

■ During World War II, 3M stopped selling Scotch Transparent Tape to civilians because the military wanted it all. At least one American munitions factory used transparent tape as a conveyor belt to move bullets.

■ Also during World War II, England's Ministry of Home

Defense used more than ten million yards of Scotch Transparent Tape on windows to minimize flying glass during air raids.

■ In 1961, 3M engineers perfected the tape so that it would never yellow or ooze adhesive. Scotch Magic Transparent Tape, with its matte finish backing, disappears when applied. It is also water resistant, and you can write on it.

■ Scotch tape has been used as an anticorrosive shield on the Goodyear blimp.

■ The Scottish tartans used to designate Scotch tapes were exclusively designed for the 3M Company by New York color consultant Arthur Allen in the 1940s.

Distribution

■ Scotch tape, the best-selling tape of any kind in the world, is found in virtually every home and office in the United States.

■ Scotch-brand tapes also include Scotch Packaging Tape, Scotch Magic Tape, and Scotch Double Stick Tape.

■ Today, 3M makes more than 300 different types of tapes.

For More Information

3M Consumer Stationery Division, Box 33594, St. Paul, MN 55133. Or telephone 1-800-364-3577.

Steel Wool Soap Pads

■ **Fill cracks in walls.** Fill cracks with pieces of an S.O.S Steel Wool Soap Pad, then plaster.

■ **Make a pincushion.** Stuff a homemade pincushion with a clean, dry, used S.O.S Steel Wool Soap Pad. The steel wool will help keep pins and needles sharp.

■ **Clean golf clubs.** Rub the golf club gently with a dry S.O.S Steel Wool Soap Pad.

■ **Clean sneakers.** Use a wet S.O.S Steel Wool Soap Pad to gently clean dirty sneakers.

■**Remove crayon from wallpaper.** Rub the crayon marks very gently with

an S.O.S Steel Wool Soap Pad, testing an inconspicuous spot first.

■ **Clean rust from a chrome car bumper.** Scrub briskly with an S.O.S Steel Wool Soap Pad.

■ **Prevent clogged drains when bathing a dog.** Place a ball made from an S.O.S Steel Wool Soap Pad in the drain opening to catch stray hairs.

■ **Tighten a screw.** Wrap a few steel strands from an S.O.S Steel Wool Soap Pad around the threads of a screw.

■ **Plug up mouse holes.** Plug small cracks and holes with S.O.S Steel Wool Soap Pads.

Invented

1913

The Name

Mrs. Edwin Cox, the inventor's wife, named the soap pads S.O.S., for "Save Our Saucepans," convinced that she had cleverly adapted the Morse code international distress signal for "Save Our Ships." In fact, the distress signal S.O.S. doesn't stand for anything. It's simply a combination of three letters represented by three identical marks (the *S* is three dots, the *O* is three dashes). The period after the last *S* was eventually deleted from the brand name in order to obtain a trademark for what would otherwise be an international distress symbol.

A Short History

In 1917, Edwin Cox, a struggling door-to-door aluminum cookware salesman in San Francisco, developed in his kitchen a steel wool scouring pad caked with dried soap as a free gift to housewives to get himself invited inside their homes to demonstrate his wares and boost sales. A few months later, demand for the soap-encrusted pads snowballed. Cox quit the aluminum cookware business and went to work for himself.

Ingredients

Steel wool, soaps, all-purpose detergents

Strange Facts

■ To prevent an S.O.S Steel Wool Soap Pad from rusting, wrap it in aluminum foil and place it in the freezer.

■ S.O.S boxes are made from 100 percent recycled paperboard, with a minimum 35 percent post-consumer content.

Distribution

■ For 75 years, S.O.S has been America's best-selling steel wool soap pads.

■ S.O.S Steel Wool Soap Pads are also available in Lemon Fresh Scent and Junior pads.

For More Information

The Clorox Company, 1221 Broadway, Oakland, CA 94612. Or telephone 1-510-271-7000.

Spray 'n Wash

■ **Remove chewing gum from hair.** Spray the gum with Spray 'n Wash, rub between fingers, comb out, then shampoo.

▫ **Clean shower tiles and doors.** Spray with Spray 'n Wash, wait three minutes, then wipe clean with a sponge.

■ **Remove varnish from hands.** Spray hands with Spray 'n Wash, rub, then wash with soap and water. Spray 'n Wash usally works better than turpentine, without burning the skin.

■ **Clean bathroom fixtures.** Spray generously with Spray 'n Wash, then shine with a cloth.

■ **Remove spots from indoor-outdoor carpeting.** Spray spots generously with Spray 'n Wash, wait five minutes, then hose down.

Invented
1970

The Name
Spray 'n Wash denotes the way this product is used. Consumers simply *spray* a garment soiled with a tough stain *and* then throw it in the *wash*.

A Short History

Herbert H. Dow founded the Dow Chemical Company with the discovery of salt deposits in northern Michigan, expanding into the research, development, and manufacture of industrial chemicals. Dow started manufacturing consumer products in 1953 with the introduction of Saran Wrap, followed by Handi-Wrap in 1960, Dow Oven Cleaner in 1963, Scrubbing Bubbles in 1966, and the Ziploc Storage Bag and Spray 'n Wash in 1970. Spray 'n Wash was introduced in an aerosol can, and in 1974, was made available in liquid form. Spray 'n Wash Stain Stick® was introduced in 1990.

Ingredients

Water, surfactant, enzymes, fragrance, stabilizers, preservative, dye

Strange Facts

■ Spray 'n Wash is nonflammable and biodegradable, has an environmentally safe propellant, and does not contain phosphorus or chlorinated solvents.

■ In 1995, Spray 'n Wash was reintroduced to the marketplace with new ergonomically designed bottles, more ef-

fective formulations, and an improved trigger sprayer.

■ In 1994, Dow became the exclusive supplier of rigid Styrofoam-brand insulation for Habitat for Humanity, a nonprofit organization that has built over 30,000 homes with the help of the hard-working, low-income families who buy the homes. As of this writing, Habitat for Humanity ranks as the seventeenth largest home builder in the United States.

■ Since 1990, Dow, in partnership with Huntsman Chemical and the U.S. National Park Service, has brought recycling to seven national parks. In 1995, nearly two million pounds of aluminum, glass, and plastics were collected in the parks, reducing the solid waste sent to landfills.

■ In 1991, the U.S. Environmental Protection Agency announced the 33/50 program, challenging companies to voluntarily reduce emissions of seventeen chemical pollutants by 33 percent by 1992, and by 50 percent by 1995. By the end of 1993, Dow had achieved a 47 percent global reduction—cutting global emissions from over 4,500 tons every year to just under 2,500 tons per year.

Distribution

■ Dow operates 130 manufacturing sites in 30 countries, and employs approximately 53,700 people around the world.

■ In 1994, DowBrands sold more than $845 million worth of consumer products.

For More Information

DowBrands L.P., P.O. Box 68511, Indianapolis, IN 46286. Or telephone 1-800-428-4795.

SueBee Honey

■ **Condition hair and prevent split ends and frizzies.** Mix one tablespoon SueBee Honey and two teaspoons Star Olive Oil. Warm the mixture (but not too hot), dip your fingers into it, and rub it into the strands of hair. Soak a towel in hot water, wring out completely, and wrap around your head for twenty minutes. Then shampoo as usual, lathering well to remove the olive oil.

■ **Give yourself a facial.** Mash a banana and add one tablespoon SueBee Honey. Cover your face with the mixture, let sit fifteen minutes, then rinse with warm water.

■ **Dress wounds and burns.** Apply SueBee Honey to the injury. Honey is hygroscopic and absorbs water, creating an environment in which disease-producing microorganisms, deprived of their moisture, cannot live.

■ **Soothe a sore throat.** Take one teaspoon of SueBee Honey at bedtime, letting it trickle down your throat.

■ **Cure a hangover.** Honey is a concentrated source of fructose. Eating SueBee Honey on crackers helps your body flush out whatever alcohol remains in the body.

■ **Relieve a cough due to a cold.** Dissolve one tablespoon SueBee Honey and one tablespoon ReaLemon in a small glass of warm water and sip it. For a stronger solution, combine equal parts SueBee Honey and ReaLemon, and take one teaspoon at bedtime. Both mixtures may help loosen phlegm.

■ **Make a bath toy.** Use an empty SueBee honey bear in the bathtub.

■ **Make a glue dispenser.** Fill a SueBee honey bear with Elmer's Glue-All and tint with food coloring to make colorful glues.

■ **Substitute honey for sugar when cooking.** Use SueBee Honey in place of granulated sugar for up to one half of the sugar. With experimentation, honey can be substituted for all the sugar in some recipes. For baked goods, add about one half teaspoon baking soda for each cup of honey used, reduce the amount of liquid in the recipe by one-quarter cup for each cup of honey used, and reduce the oven temperature by 25°F to prevent overbrowning. For easy removal, spray measuring cup with Pam No Stick Cooking Spray before adding honey.

■ **Make children sleepy at bedtime and help prevent small children from wetting the bed.** A teaspoon of honey at bedtime will act as a sedative to a child's nervous system and will attract and hold fluid in a child's body during the hours of sleeping. When a child over one year is given honey, the blood and tissue calcium begins to increase. The calcium unites with excess phosphorous to form a compound that makes bones, teeth, hair, and fingernails. The sedative effect on the nervous system of a child may be observed within an hour. Honey should not be fed to infants under one year of age. Honey is a safe and wholesome food for older children and adults.

■ **Help heal erysipelas.** Generously cover the affected area with honey, then cover with cotton for 24 hours. Repeat if necessary.

Invented
Between 10 and 20 million B.C.

The Name
SueBee is a combination of the misspelled word *Sioux*, the Indian tribe for which Sioux City, Iowa, is named, and the word *Bee*, the insect that makes honey.

A Short History
Honey is the sweet liquid produced by bees from flower nectar. The source of the nectar determines the color and flavor of the honey. Most honey in the United States is produced from clover or alfalfa, yielding light-colored and delicately flavored honeys. Other common honeys are made from basswood, buckwheat, eucalyptus, fireweed, orange

blossom, sage, tulip poplar, tupelo, and wildflower. Honeycombs are harvested, placed in honey extractors that whirl the honeycombs around, forcing the honey out. After the honey is extracted, it is pasteurized, strained, filtered, and vacuum-packed into jars, poured into squeezable bottles, or "spun" and packed in serving tubs.

In 1921, in Sioux City, Iowa, five men pooled $200 and three thousand pounds of honey to create the Sioux Honey Association. Today, hundreds of members market their honey worldwide through the Association, which oversees the consistent flavor and premium quality of SueBee Honey.

Ingredient
U.S. Grade A white pure honey

Strange Facts

■ In ancient times, women were advised to put honey in their vaginas for contraceptive purposes. The stickiness was thought to prevent sperm from entering the uterus. It doesn't.

■ Anthropologists believe that ancient Egyptians used honey in embalming and to feed to sacred animals.

■ Honey is alluded to in the Sumerian and Babylonian cuneiform writings, the Hittite code, the sacred writings of India, the Vedas, and in Chinese manuscripts. In the Bible, Israel is called "the land of milk and honey." Egyptian tomb reliefs from the third century B.C. depict workers collecting honey from hives, and archaeologist T. M. Davies discovered a 3,300-year-old jar of honey in an Egyptian tomb.

■ In ancient Greece, mead, an alcoholic beverage made with honey, was considered the drink of the Greek gods.

- Honey contains more nutrients than refined sugars, including traces of thiamin, riboflavin, niacin, pantothenic acid, vitamin B_6, vitamin C, calcium, copper, iron, magnesium, manganese, phosphorus, potassium, sodium, and zinc.

- Since honey absorbs and retains moisture, it is commonly used in the baking industry to keep baked goods moist and fresh. Honey's high sugar content and acidity make it an excellent food preservative and sweetener. Honey's unique properties also enhance salad dressings, sauces, candies, dairy products, spreads, fillings, cereals, cured meats, beverages, and snack foods.

- Vegans are strict vegetarians who eat only foods from plants, avoiding all animal flesh and animal products, including milk, cheese, eggs, and honey.

- The proverb "More flies are taken with a drop of honey than a ton of vinegar" first appeared in *Gnomologia* by Thomas Fuller in 1732.

- Beekeepers are called apiarists.

- The queen bee is the only sexually developed female in the hive. Worker bees (sexually undeveloped females) select a two-day-old larva to be the queen. She emerges from her cell eleven days later to mate in flight with approximately eighteen drone bees (males), receiving several million sperm cells, which last her two-year life span. The queen starts to lay eggs about ten days after mating. A productive queen can lay three thousand eggs in a single day.

- The honey bee's distinctive buzz is actually the sound of its wings stroking 11,400 times per minute.

- "If you want to gather honey," said President Abraham Lincoln, "don't kick over the beehive."

- The scotch liqueur Drambuie is made with honey.

- "The only reason for being a bee that I know of is making

honey," said Winnie the Pooh in *The House at Pooh Corner* by A. A. Milne. "And the only reason for making honey is so I can eat it."

■ Store honey at room temperature away from direct sunlight. Refrigeration speeds crystallization. To avoid sticky drips, place honey jars and bottles on a saucer or disposable coaster.

■ Honey never spoils. Crystallization does not affect the taste or purity of honey. If honey crystallizes, just pop it in warm water or in the microwave in a microwave-safe container on high for one to three minutes, stirring every thirty seconds.

Distribution

■ SueBee Honey is the only nationally advertised brand of honey in the United States, and the Sioux Honey Association is the largest honey marketing organization in the world.

■ In 1994, more than 217 million pounds of honey were produced in the United States, valued at $111 million.

■ The International Trade Commission estimates that there are about 211,600 beekeepers in the United States. An estimated 200,000 are hobbyists with less than twenty-five hives. The approximately 2,000 commercial beekeeping operations in the United States (with over three hundred hives each) produce about 60 percent of the nation's honey.

■ Many commercial beekeepers rent out their colonies during the year to pollinate crops for farmers. The U.S. Department of Agriculture estimates that about 2.8 million acres of almonds, apples, melons, plums, avocados, blueberries, cherries, cucumbers, pears, cranberries, kiwi, and other major crops in the United States depend on insect pollination from honeybees.

■ Utah is known as the beehive state, despite the fact that in 1994, North Dakota led the nation in honey production with more than 32 million pounds, followed by South Dakota, California, and Florida with more than 19 million pounds each.

■ The National Honey Board's honey bear logo appears on over 390 food products that contain high levels of pure honey used according to the board's strict standards.

■ Every year the average American consumes 1.1 pounds of honey. That's one honey bear per person. To make one pound of honey, a hive of bees must tap two million flowers, flying over 55,000 miles. The average worker honey bee makes one-twelfth teaspoon of honey in her lifetime, flying about fifteen miles per hour and visiting between fifty and one hundred flowers in each collection trip.

■ SueBee makes Clover Honey, Sunflower Honey, Natural Pure Honey, Orange Honey, Sage Honey, Spun Honey, Aunt Sue's Raw Honey, Squeeze Bears, Premium Barbecue Sauce, and Louisiana Style Premium Barbecue Sauce. Sue-Bee Honey also packages a variety of Private Label products including Clover Maid, Super G, Fred Meyer, Grand Union, Stop & Shop, Western Family, Village Park, National, and North American.

■ For a free copy of the National Honey Board's new 96-page honey-inspired cookbook, *Sweetened with Honey*, send your name and address, along with a check or money order for $2.50 to cover postage and handling to: National Honey Board, Dept. C, P.O. Box 7760, Marshfield, WI 54449. Allow four to six weeks for delivery.

For More Information

■ Sioux Honey Association, P.O. Box 388, Sioux City, Iowa 51102. Or telephone 1-712-258-0638.

■ National Honey Board, 390 Lashley Street, Longmont, CO 80501-6010. Or telephone 1-800-553-7162.

Pepper Sauce

■ **Control spider mites, whiteflies, aphids, and thrips on houseplants.** Purée two teaspoons Tabasco pepper sauce and three cloves garlic in a blender; add three cups water and two tablespoons biodegradable liquid detergent, then strain into a spray bottle and coat the leaves of the plant.

■ **Combat the common cold.** Mix ten to twenty drops Tabasco pepper sauce in a glass of tomato juice. Drink several of these decongestant tonics daily to help relieve congestion in the nose, sinuses, and lungs. Or gargle with ten to twenty drops Tabasco pepper sauce mixed in a glass of water to clear out the respiratory tract.

■ **Prevent cats from scratching dark woodwork.** Rub the area with Tabasco pepper sauce and buff thoroughly. The faint smell of Tabasco pepper sauce repels cats.

■ **Make spicy popcorn.** Add a few drops of Tabasco pepper sauce to the cooking oil before adding the popcorn kernels.

■ **Make a Bloody Mary.** Combine one quart tomato juice, one cup vodka, one tablespoon fresh lime or lemon juice, one tablespoon Worcestershire sauce, one teaspoon salt, and one-quarter teaspoon Tabasco pepper sauce in a two-quart pitcher. Stir well, chill, and serve over ice, garnished with a slice of lime.

■ **Make a Cola Volcano.** Mix one or two drops Tabasco pepper sauce to a glass of Coca-Cola, stir well, and add ice.

■ **Cook with Tabasco pepper sauce.** *The Tabasco Cookbook* by Paul McIlhenny with Barbara Hunter suggests recipes for Frog Legs Piquant, Cheese Scones, and Spiced Peaches—all with Tabasco pepper sauce.

■ **Relieve a toothache.** Apply a dab of Tabasco pepper sauce to the gum.

Invented
1868

The Name
Tabasco, a name of Central American Indian origin, was chosen by creator Edmund McIlhenny because he liked the sound of the word.

A Short History
In 1862, when Union troops entered New Orleans, Edmund McIlhenny, a successful banker, fled with his wife, Mary

Avery McIlhenny, to Baton Rouge and then to Avery Island, an island of solid salt approximately 140 miles west of New Orleans and the site of America's first salt mine. In 1863, Union forces invaded the island, destroyed the salt mines, and the McIlhennys fled to Texas.

After the Civil War, Edmund McIlhenny returned to Avery Island to find his wife's family plantation plundered but some capsicum hot peppers surviving. Determined to turn the peppers into income, McIlhenny made a pepper sauce by mixing crushed peppers and salt in crockery jars and letting the concoction age for thirty days. He then added "the best French wine vinegar" and let the mixture age for another thirty days. He strained the sauce, filled several small cologne bottles and sent the sauce to friends. In 1868, McIlhenny sent 350 bottles of his pepper sauce, under the trademark Tabasco, to a carefully selected group of wholesalers, and a year later, he sold several thousand bottles at a dollar each. The company is family-run to this very day.

Ingredients

Vinegar, aged red pepper, salt

Strange Facts

■ Tabasco pepper sauce is made from a species of pepper called *Capsicum frutescens*, known for centuries in Latin America and first recorded in 1493 by Dr. Chauca, the physician on Columbus's voyage.

■ Capsicum peppers contain an alkaloid called capsaicin, a spicy compound found in no other plant.

■ In 1912, pharmacologist Wilbur Scoville devised an organoleptic test to rate the hotness of peppers. The mildest bell peppers rate zero; habaneros peppers score 200,000 to 300,000 units. Tabasco pepper sauce scores between 9,000 to 12,000 units on the Scoville scale.

■ Tabasco pepper sauce is still made much the same way Edmund McIlhenny first developed the sauce. Ripe peppers are harvested, crushed, mixed with Avery Island salt, and aged in white oak barrels for up to three years. The peppers are then drained, blended with strong, all-natural vinegar, stirred for several weeks, strained, bottled, and shipped.

■ Harvard University's Hasty Pudding Club produced *Burlesque Opera of Tabasco* in 1893 with the approval of Edmund McIlhenny's son, John Avery McIlhenny, who bought the rights to the production and had it staged in New York City.

■ In 1898, Lord Horatio Herbert Kitchener's troops brought Tabasco pepper sauce on their invasion of Khartoum in the Sudan.

■ In the 1920s, Fernand Petiot, an American working at Harry's Bar in Paris, created the Bloody Mary. Tabasco pepper sauce was added to the recipe in the 1930s at the King Cole Bar in New York's St. Regis Hotel.

■ In 1932, when the British government began an isolationist "Buy British" campaign, Parliament banned the purchase of Tabasco pepper sauce, popular in England since 1868 and available in the House of Commons dining rooms. The resulting protest from members of Parliament was dubbed "the Tabasco Tempest," and inevitably Tabasco pepper sauce returned to parliamentary tables. To this day Queen Elizabeth uses Tabasco pepper sauce on her lobster cocktail.

■ During the Vietnam War, McIlhenny Company sent thousands of copies of the *Charley Ration Cookbook*, filled with recipes for spicing up C-rations with Tabasco pepper sauce, wrapped around two-ounce bottles of Tabasco pepper sauce in waterproof canisters.

■ Former president George Bush is a Tabasco pepper sauce devotee, sprinkling the sauce on tuna fish sandwiches, eggs, and fried pork rinds. After receiving the Republican nomination for President in 1988, Bush handed out personalized bottles of Tabasco pepper sauce as presents for members of his family who dined with him at Arnaud's Restaurant in New Orleans. "I love hot sauce," Bush told *Time* magazine in 1992, "I splash Tabasco all over."

■ During Operation Desert Storm, a miniature bottle of Tabasco pepper sauce was included in one out of every three ration kits sent to troops in the Gulf. The United States military now packs Tabasco pepper sauce in every ration kit.

■ Over 100,000 people visit Avery Island each year to see Tabasco pepper sauce being made and visit the Tabasco Country Store. Each visitor receives a miniature bottle of Tabasco pepper sauce and a handful of recipes.

■ For a free catalogue filled with Tabasco and McIlhenny Farms products, assorted cookbooks, giftware, and Cajun specialties, telephone 1-800-634-9599.

Distribution

■ McIlhenny Company sells more than 100 million bottles of Tabasco pepper sauce a year.

■ Tabasco pepper sauce bottles are labeled in nineteen languages and shipped to more than one hundred countries.

■ Americans use more Tabasco pepper sauce than any other nation, followed by the Japanese, who sprinkle it on pizza and spaghetti.

■ McIlhenny Company produced all its peppers on Avery

Island until the late 1960s. Now, more than 90 percent of the pepper crop is grown and harvested under the company's direct supervision in Honduras, Colombia, Venezuela, Dominican Republic, Costa Rica, and Ecuador.

■ Food critic Craig Claiborne claims that "Tabasco sauce is as basic as mother's milk."

For More Information

McIlhenny Company, Avery Island, LA 70513-5002. Or telephone 1-800-634-9599.

Turtle Wax

■ **Lubricate furniture drawers and windows.** Apply Turtle Wax on the casters of drawers and windows so they slide open and shut easily.

■ **Make bumper stickers easy to remove.** Apply Turtle Wax to the spot before applying the bumper sticker, thus assuring that the bumper sticker will peel away with much greater ease within a month.

■ **Polish leather shoes.** Dab on Turtle Wax and shine with a clean, soft cloth.

■ **Make a swing set sliding board more slippery.** Cover with two coats of Turtle Wax, polishing between applications.

■ **Polish Formica or plastic tabletops.** A coat of Turtle Wax rejuvenates dulled plastic tabletops and counters.

■ **Prevent snow from sticking to a shovel.** Cover the shovel with two thick coats of Turtle Wax.

■ **Remove the white rings from furniture.** Apply Turtle Wax to the ring with your finger.

■ **Prevent playing cards from sticking together.** Wax the backs of the cards with Turtle Wax and rub with a soft cloth.

■ **Help dust and dirt slide off a dustpan.** Put a coat of Turtle Wax on the dustpan.

■ **Clean and refinish your bathtub.** Rub Turtle Wax into the tub, tiles, and faucets with a soft cloth, and polish immediately with a clean cloth or an electric buffer before the wax dries.

■ **Prevent tools from rusting.** Lightly coat tools with Turtle Wax.

Invented

1945

The Name

While driving from Beloit, Wisconsin, company founder Benjamin Hirsch, the developer of Plastone car polish, stopped at a place named Turtle Creek, rested by a stream, and was struck by his reflection in the water. Realizing that his car polish provided a wax coating as tough as a turtle shell and as reflective as Turtle Creek, he renamed his product Turtle Wax.

A Short History

In 1945, with just $500, ex-magician Benjamin Hirsch set up shop in a small Chicago storefront at 2207 Chicago Avenue, where he developed Plastone Liquid Car Polish by mixing batches in a bathtub. His wife and partner, Marie, would bottle the polish, and Ben would sell it. His best sales technique was to wax parked cars while waiting for the owners to return. In the early 1950s, after a sales call in Beloit, Wisconsin, Ben took a stroll along Turtle Creek, and shortly after, Liquid Plastone Car Polish became Turtle Wax with the hard shell finish. Today, the Hirsches' daughter, Sondra, and her husband, Denis Healy, run the company.

Ingredients

Silicones, polishing agents, water, thickeners, petroleum distillates, preservatives, coloring

Strange Fact

■ Turtle Wax, Inc., is frequently offered supplies of turtles. Former company president Carl Schmid would refuse these offers politely and point out that the turtles in Turtle Wax are like the horses in horseradish.

Distribution

■ Turtle Wax is the world's largest-selling car wax.

■ Turtle Wax also makes car polishes, car washes, protectants, velour cleaner, upholstery cleaner, carpet cleaner, spot remover, wheel cleaners, chrome polish, rubbing compound, polishing compound, bug and tar remover, and de-icer.

For More Information

Turtle Wax, Inc., 5655 West 73rd Street, Chicago, IL 60638. Or telephone 1-708-563-3600.

20 Mule Team

Borax

■ **Preserve flowers.** Mix one part 20 Mule Team Borax and two parts cornmeal. Fill the bottom one inch of an empty airtight canister with the mixture. Place the flower on the mixture, then gently cover the flower with more mixture, being careful not to crush the flower or distort the petals. Flowers with a lot of overlapping petals, such as roses and carnations, are best treated by sprinkling mixture directly into the blossom before placing them into the box. Seal the canister and store at room temperature in a dry place for seven to ten days. When the flowers are dried, pour off the mixture and dust the flowers with a soft artist's brush. Borax removes the moisture from blossoms and leaves, preventing the wilting that would normally result.

■ **Shine china.** Add one-half cup 20 Mule Team Borax to a sinkful of warm water, rinse fine china, then rinse again in clean water.

■ **Deodorize cat filler.** Mix one-and-a-half cups 20 Mule Team Borax to every five pounds of cat filler to reduce and control odor in the cat box.

■ **Clean hairbrushes and combs.** Mix a quarter cup 20 Mule Team Borax and a tablespoon of Dawn dishwashing detergent in a basin of warm water. Soak hairbrushes and combs in the solution, rinse clean, and dry.

■ **Clean a metal coffeepot.** Fill the percolator with water and add one teaspoon 20 Mule Team Borax and one teaspoon detergent powder. Boil the water, let the mixture sit for a few minutes, then rinse clean.

■ **Clean chocolate from clothing.** Sponge the spot with a solution of one tablespoon 20 Mule Team Borax and one cup warm water. Flush with water. If that doesn't work, make a paste with borax and water, work into the stain, let set for one hour, flush well with warm water, and launder as usual.

■ **Make children's clothing flame retardant.** Mix together nine ounces 20 Mule Team Borax and four ounces boric acid in one gallon water. If the article is washable, soak in the solution after the final rinsing, then dry. If the garment is not washable, spray with the solution. This solution, recommended by fire departments, may wash out of clothing and should be used after each washing or dry cleaning.

■ Make your own household cleanser for walls and floors. Add one-half cup 20 Mule Team Borax, one-half teaspoon Dawn dishwashing liquid, and one teaspoon ammonia to two gallons warm water.

■ Make your own automatic dishwashing soap. Use equal parts 20 Mule Team Borax and washing soda.

■ Gently clean porcelain and aluminum cookware. Sprinkle 20 Mule Team Borax on pots and pans, rub with a damp dishcloth, and rinse thoroughly.

■ Reduce water spots on glasses and dishes. Add one tablespoon 20 Mule Team Borax to the dishwasher.

■ Clean spills and stains on carpet and upholstery. Blot up the spill, sprinkle 20 Mule Team Borax to cover the area, let dry, and vacuum. Before treating, make sure the carpet dye is colorfast by testing an unexposed area with a paste of 20 Mule Team Borax and water. For wine and alcohol stains, dissolve one cup 20 Mule Team Borax in one quart water. Sponge in the solution, wait thirty minutes, shampoo the spotted area, let dry, and vacuum.

■ Deodorize garbage disposals. Sprinkle two to three tablespoons 20 Mule Team Borax in the drain, let it stand for fifteen minutes, then flush with water with the disposal on. Borax helps deodorize garbage disposals by neutralizing acidic odors.

■ **Neutralize urine odors from mattresses and mattress covers.** Dampen the spot, rub in 20 Mule Team Borax, let dry, then vacuum or brush clean.

■ **Neutralize pet urine and sour spilled milk odors.** Dampen the spot, rub in 20 Mule Team Borax, let dry, then vacuum or brush clean.

■ **Boost laundry detergent.** Add one-half cup 20 Mule Team Borax to each wash load along with the recommended amount of detergent. For large capacity and front-loading machines, add three-quarters cup. Borax acts as a water conditioner, boosting the cleaning power of detergent by controlling alkalinity, deodorizing the clothes, and aiding the removal of stains and soil.

■ **Wash diapers and baby clothes.** Flush out dirty diapers and soak as soon as possible in a diaper pail filled with warm water and one-half cup 20 Mule Team Borax. Presoak for at least thirty minutes before washing in warm water, adding one-half cup Borax with the recommended amount of detergent. Wash linens, bibs, slips, and cotton crib liners in hot water, adding one-half cup 20 Mule Team Borax and detergent. Borax helps get rid of odors, reduce staining, and make diapers more absorbent.

■ **Wash delicate hand washables.** Dissolve one-quarter cup 20 Mule Team Borax and two tablespoons detergent in a basin of warm water. Soak hand washables for ten minutes, rinse in clear, cool water, blot with a towel, lay flat (woolens) or hang to dry (away from sunlight and direct heat).

■ **Eliminate bathtub rust stains.** Scrub the stains with a paste made from 20 Mule Team Borax and ReaLemon lemon juice.

■ **Soften soap and rinse waters.** Add one tablespoon 20 Mule Team Borax per quart of water.

■ **Clean and deodorize a refrigerator.** Mix one tablespoon 20 Mule Team Borax in one quart warm water. Wash spilled food with a sponge and soft cloth. Rinse with cold water.

■ **Keep the water in a humidifier free from odor.** Dissolve one tablespoon 20 Mule Team Borax per gallon of water before adding to the unit. Use this treatment once or twice a year.

■ **Wash windows.** Mix one-quarter cup 20 Mule Team Borax, one-half cup ammonia, and two gallons water to add more sparkle when cleaning windows.

■ **Reduce ash and eliminate smoke problems from candlewicks in homemade candles.** Dissolve one tablespoon table salt and three tablespoons 20 Mule Team Borax in one cup warm water. Soak heavy twine in the solution for at least twenty-four hours. Allow the twine to dry thoroughly before using to make candles.

Invented
1891

The Name

20 Mule Team Borax is named for the twenty-mule teams used to transport borax from the mines in Death Valley during the late nineteenth century. The word *borax* derives from the Arabic *buraq* or *baurach*, which means to glitter or shine.

A Short History

Borax, a naturally occurring mineral composed of sodium, boron, oxygen, and water, was mined in 2000 B.C. from salt lakes in Tibet and Kashmir. It has been used in pottery glazes since the Middle Ages and was brought to Europe by Arabs. Borax is generally found embedded deep in the ground, along with clay and other substances. In 1881, borax deposits were discovered in Death Valley, California. W. T. Coleman, a San Francisco–based sales agent for borax producer F. M. "Borax" Smith, promptly acquired the discovery site and other nearby properties, including one near Furnace Creek where he established the Harmony Borax Works. Beginning in 1883, famous 100-foot-long twenty-mule teams hauled Coleman's borax 165 miles across the desert from Death Valley to the nearest train depot in Mojave. The twenty-day round trip started 190 feet below sea level and climbed to an elevation of over 2,000 feet before it was over.

In 1890, "Borax" Smith acquired Coleman's borax properties and established the Pacific Coast Borax Company, using Coleman's "Twenty-Mule Team" as the brand name for its "99 1/2% pure" borax. In 1886, Smith joined with a British chemical firm to form Pacific Coast Borax and Redwood's Chemical Works, Ltd., which formed Borax Consolidated, Ltd. London-based RZT Corporation (formerly Rio Tinto-Zinc), the world's largest mining concern, acquired Borax in 1968. Twenty years later, 20 Mule Team Borax, Borateem bleach, and Boraxo brand soap were sold to the Dial Corporation.

Ingredient
Borax

Strange Facts

■ Despite changes in packaging, 20 Mule Team Borax has remained unchanged for over 100 years.

■ In some cases, the twenty-mule teams of Death Valley actually consisted of eighteen mules and two horses.

■ Between 1883 and 1889, the twenty-mule teams hauled more than twenty million pounds of borax out of Death Valley. During this time, not a single animal was lost nor did a single wagon break down.

■ Today it would take more than 250 mule teams to transport the borax ore processed in just one day at Borax's modern facility in the Mojave Desert.

■ Although the mule teams were replaced by railroad cars in 1889, twenty-mule teams continued to make promotional and ceremonial appearances at events ranging from the 1904 St. Louis World's Fair to President Woodrow Wilson's inauguration in 1916. They won first place in the 1917 Pasadena Rose Parade and attended the dedication of the San Francisco Bay Bridge in 1937.

■ In 1940, MGM produced *Twenty Mule Team*, a popular movie that was promoted by a forty-city mule-team tour.

The film starred Wallace Beery, Leo Carrillo, and Anne Baxter.

■ Borax is used in the manufacture of glass and ceramic glazes, fire-retardant textiles and wood, and photographic developers.

■ Since boron is important in the calcium cycle of plants, borax is often added to boron-poor soils as a fertilizer.

■ Borax deposits in Death Valley were abandoned when richer deposits were found elsewhere in the Mojave Desert, turning mining settlements into ghost towns that now help make the region a tourist attraction.

■ Borax retards flames because it melts at a low temperature and blocks the diffusion of oxygen to the burning surface.

■ According to legend, borax was used by Egyptians in mummification.

■ In the furniture business, the word *borax* signifies cheap, mass-produced furniture.

■ Adding borax to hard water precipitates mineral salts.

■ 20 Mule Team Borax was once proclaimed a "miracle mineral" and was used to aid digestion, keep milk sweet, improve the complexion, remove dandruff, and even cure epilepsy.

■ Borax sponsored *Death Valley Days*, first on radio and later on television. This program became the longest-running serial in American broadcasting history.

Distribution

■ Borax conducts mining operations at Boron in California's Mojave Desert and at four sites in the Argentine Andes.

■ Most of the world's supply of borates comes from Boron, California, and from Turkey.

- Borax's mine in Boron supplies more than half of the world's borax.
- The Dial Corporation operates thirteen manufacturing plants in the United States and one in Mexico.
- The Dial Corporation also makes Dial Soap, the best-selling deodorant soap in the United States.

For More Information

- The Dial Corp., Consumer Information Center, 15101 North Scottsdale Road, Scottsdale, AZ 85254. Or telephone 1-800-528-0849.
- U.S. Borax Inc., 26877 Tourney Road, Valencia, CA 91355-1847. Or telephone 1-805-287-5400.

Vanilla Extract

■ **Perfume yourself.** A dab of McCormick/Schilling Pure Vanilla Extract behind each ear makes a delightful fragrance.

■ **Eliminate paint odor.** Mix two teaspoons McCormick/Schilling Pure Vanilla Extract per gallon of paint.

■ **Flavor Alka-Seltzer.** Add a few drops of McCormick/Schilling Pure Vanilla Extract and one teaspoon sugar to a glass of Alka-Seltzer to improve the taste.

■ **Eliminate odors in the refrigerator.** Pour a few drops of McCormick/Schilling Pure Vanilla Extract on a cotton ball and place it on a saucer in the refrigerator.

■ **Deodorize a cooler.** Wash out the cooler with a solution of three-quarters cup Clorox bleach per gallon of hot water, then saturate a cloth with McCormick/Schilling Pure Vanilla Extract and wipe down the insides.

Invented
Unknown

The Name
Vanilla extract is the extract from the vanilla bean, prepared by chopping the beans into small pieces and then percolating them with alcohol and water.

A Short History
Vanilla beans, the fruit of a unique species of orchid with aerial roots, fruit pods, and fragrant flowers, is native to the tropical rain forests of Mexico and Central America. Indigenous natives discovered that the tasteless and odorless vanilla bean, when dried by months of tropical heat and humidity, produced a rich taste and aroma. When Aztecs conquered the Indian nations of southeastern Mexico in the 1500s, they named the vanilla bean *tlilxochitl*. In 1520, Aztec emperor Montezuma served Spanish explorer Hernán Cortez a thick, syrupy mixture of cocoa beans, ground corn, honey, and black vanilla pods in a golden

goblet. Cortez conquered the Aztecs, killed Montezuma, and brought vanilla to Europe, where it achieved great popularity. Today, vanilla beans are grown primarily in Madagascar, Indonesia, Tahiti, and Mexico.

Ingredients

Vanilla bean extractives in water, alcohol (35 percent), and sugar

Strange Facts

■ The word *vanilla* stems from the Latin word *vagina*, perhaps because vanilla fruit pods vaguely resemble a sheath or possibly because vanilla was considered an aphrodisiac.

■ Vanilla is the world's most popular flavor.

■ The vanilla bean requires approximately nine months to reach maturity, growing six to ten inches long like an overgrown string bean. Harvested beans are immersed in a hot-water bath, then put into wooden boxes and covered with blankets to lock in the heat, where they will "sweat" for 24 to 72 hours, beginning the enzymatic change that produces vanillin. Finally, the beans are placed on blankets and dried in the sun for three to four months to complete the curing process. The cured beans—wrinkled and chocolate colored—are tied in bundles, packed in boxes, and shipped to McCormick, where they are weighed, chopped, and percolated in large stainless steel containers much like coffee percolators. After the vanilla is aged for several weeks, it is bottled and shipped to stores.

■ The Totonac Indians of Mexico discovered how to hand-pollinate the vanilla orchid, which flowers for only one day.

- Vanilla is the second most expensive flavoring in the world to produce, preceded only by saffron.
- Queen Elizabeth I loved vanilla so much that she eventually refused all foods prepared without it.
- Thomas Jefferson, having acquired a taste for vanilla in France, was the first person to import it to the United States.
- The vanilla orchid is the only orchid known to bear edible fruit.

Distribution

- McCormick products are distributed under the Schilling label in the western United States.
- Vanilla is the foremost flavor in ice cream, puddings, cakes, chocolates, baked goods, syrups, candies, liqueurs, tobacco, and soft drinks. Vanilla tincture is also used in perfumes.

For More Information

McCormick & Company, Inc., P.O. Box 208, Hunt Valley, MD 21030-0208.

Ultra Paper Towels

■ **Remove crayon from a chalkboard.** Place a VIVA Ultra paper towel over the crayon marks and press the paper towel with a warm iron. The iron will melt the crayon wax as the paper towel absorbs it.

■ **Make an impromptu coffee filter.** Use a VIVA Ultra paper towel in the coffeemaker.

■ **Absorb excess oil from a sewing machine.** After oiling your sewing machine, stitch several rows on a VIVA Ultra paper towel before sewing any fabric.

■ **Keep vegetables fresher longer.** Line the bottom of the vegetable bin in your refrigerator with VIVA Ultra paper towels to absorb the excess moisture.

■ **Strain the fat from broth.** Strain the broth through a VIVA Ultra paper towel.

■ **Prevent the wet pages of a book from wrinkling.** Place a VIVA Ultra paper towel between every wet page, close the book, place a heavy book on top, and let it sit overnight.

■ **Remove candle wax from carpet or upholstery.** Place a VIVA Ultra paper towel over the wax. Gently press the paper towel with a warm iron. The iron will melt the wax and the paper towel will absorb it.

■ **De-silk an ear of corn.** Shuck an ear of corn, then wipe it in a single stroke from top to bottom with a dampened VIVA Ultra paper towel.

■ **Prevent cast-iron skillets from rusting.** Place a VIVA Ultra paper towel between your cast-iron pots and pans in the cupboard. VIVA absorbs the moisture that can promote rust.

■ **Sprout seeds before planting.** Cut a three-inch strip from a VIVA Ultra paper towel, dampen it, and lay it on top of a strip of Saran Wrap. Place the seeds on top of the paper towel at the intervals recommended on the seed packet. Cover with another strip of damp VIVA Ultra paper towel, then roll the paper and plastic together, place in a Baggie, and store in a warm place. When the roots begin to sprout, remove the Baggie, unroll the Saran Wrap, plant the strip of VIVA Ultra paper towel in a well-tilled garden bed, cover with a fine layer of soil, and water thoroughly. The VIVA Ultra paper towel acts as a mulch to inhibit dehydration and soon dissolves, ensuring a perfectly spaced row of seedlings.

Invented
1967

The Name
VIVA, the Spanish word for *live*, apparently signifies the paper towel's longevity. Ultra alludes to the paper towel's additional strength and absorbency.

A Short History
In 1879, brothers Clarence and Irvin Scott founded the Scott Paper Company and began selling paper bags out of push-carts on the streets of Philadelphia. Capitalizing on the growth of indoor plumbing in the late nineteenth century, Scott started making toilet paper, supplying more than 2,000 customers by the turn of century. In 1902, the company introduced its first brand-name toilet paper, trademarked Waldorf, followed in 1914 by ScotTissue, supported by the company's first advertising campaign. Print ads featured a small boy declaring, "They have a pretty house, Mother, but their bathroom paper hurts."

In 1907, unsanitary conditions in Philadelphia school-rooms, where teachers used cloth towels to clean bathroom mishaps, prompted the Scott Paper Company to invent the paper towel. The company introduced the paper towel roll under the ScotTissue brand in 1931 and later invented perforated embossing to add softness and absorbency.

Scott Paper introduced VIVA paper towels in 1967. In 1995, Kimberly-Clark, the maker of Kotex tampons, Huggies disposable diapers, and Kleenex tissues, bought Scott Paper for $7.4 billion.

Ingredients
Processed wood pulp, wet-strength resin, paper ink, adhesive

Strange Facts
■ Kimberly-Clark owns about 700,000 acres of timberland, and also makes disposable surgical gowns, sterile wrapping for surgical instruments, and groundwood printing papers and paper specialty products for the tobacco and electronics industries.

■ From its corporate flight department, Kimberly-Clark set up Milwaukee-based regional airline Midwest Express in 1984 to transport its employees. Kimberly-Clark sold its interest in the airline in public offerings in 1995 and 1996.

■ VIVA Ultra paper towels are made from both long and short wood fibers. The long fibers are obtained from soft-wood trees, such as pine and spruce, and are used primarily for strength. The short fibers are obtained from hardwood trees, such as oak and maple, and are used primarily for softness.

Distribution

■ Kimberly-Clark also makes Huggies baby wipes, Kleenex tissues, Huggies disposable diapers, Kotex, New Freedom, and Depend.

■ Kimberly-Clark has plants in the U.S. and 25 foreign countries. Its products are sold in 150 countries.

For More Information

Kimberly-Clark Corporation, 401 North Lake Street, P.O. Box 349, Neenah, WI 54957-0349. Or telephone 1-800-272-6882.

Corn Oil

■ **Moisturize skin.** Massage Wesson Corn Oil into your skin, wait fifteen minutes, remove the excess oil with paper towels, then take a hot bath.

■ **Make bubble bath.** Mix two cups Wesson Corn Oil, three tablespoons of liquid shampoo, and one-quarter teaspoon your favorite perfume. Mix the solution in a blender at high speed.

■ **Prevent cat hair balls.** Add a teaspoon of Wesson Corn Oil to one cat meal daily.

■ **Add a shine to your dog's coat.** Add a teaspoon of Wesson Corn Oil to each food serving.

■ **Condition hair.** Massage lukewarm Wesson Corn Oil into dry hair, cover hair with a shower cap for thirty minutes, then shampoo and rinse thoroughly.

■ **Remove oil-based paint from skin.** Use Wesson Corn Oil instead of turpentine.

■ **Season a cast-iron skillet.** Rub a drop of Wesson Corn Oil on the inside of the pan to keep it seasoned. Place a paper towel over and under the skillet when storing. To season a new cast-iron skillet, grease with unsalted Wesson Corn Oil and warm in an oven for two hours. Repeat after washing the skillet for several weeks.

■ **Remove rust spots from a cast-iron skillet.** Apply Wesson Corn Oil, let stand, then wipe thoroughly. Repeat if necessary.

■ **Prevent car doors from freezing in winter.** Rub the gaskets with Wesson Corn Oil to seal out water without harming the gaskets.

■ **Remove white spots or watermarks from wood furniture.** Dip a cloth in Wesson Corn Oil, then into cigar or cigarette ashes. Rub with the grain, across the spot, until it disappears.

■ **Prevent snow from sticking to a shovel.** Coat the shovel with Wesson Corn Oil.

■ **Remove decals.** Saturate the decal with Wesson Corn Oil.

■ **Oil wooden spoons, cutting boards, and butcher blocks.** Put Wesson Corn Oil on a paper towel, rub it into the wood, then wipe clean.

■ **Soothe tired feet.** Rub warmed Wesson Corn Oil into your feet, wrap in a damp, hot towel, and sit for ten minutes.

■ **Remove glue from furniture.** Apply a dab of Wesson Corn Oil and rub.

■ **Remove a splinter.** Soak the wounded area in Wesson Corn Oil for a few minutes to soften the skin before trying to remove the splinter.

■ **Break in a new baseball mitt.** Rub a few drops of Wesson Corn Oil into the palm of the glove, place a baseball in the glove, fold the mitt around it, and secure with rubber bands. Tuck the mitt under a mattress and leave overnight.

■ **Remove burrs, tar, and sticky substances from a dog's hair.** Saturate the area with Wesson Corn Oil. Wash with dog shampoo, rinse immediately, and brush clean.

■ **Clean the sap from a Christmas tree from your hands.** Rub your hands with Wesson Corn Oil and wipe clean with a paper towel.

■ **Remove price tags from appliances or the price-tag sheet from an automobile.** Apply Wesson Corn Oil. Let sit and then scrape away.

■ **Make cleaning a barbecue grill easy.** Before cooking, coat the grill with Wesson Corn Oil. Clean when the grill is cool to the touch.

■ **Remove paper stuck to a wood surface.** Saturate the

paper with Wesson Corn Oil, let sit for a while, and gently peel the paper off.

■ **Keep your sink shining.** Wipe the sink with a few drops of Wesson Corn Oil on a soft cloth.

■ **Treat ear mites in cats.** Put a few drops of Wesson Corn Oil into your cat's ear and massage. Then clean out all debris with a ball of cotton. Repeat daily for three days, and the mites should be gone. The oil soothes the cat's sensitive skin, smothers the mites, and promotes healing.

Invented
1899

The Name
Wesson Corn Oil is named after company founder Dr. David Wesson.

A Short History
In 1899, Dr. David Wesson, a plant chemist with the Southern Cotton Oil Company in Savannah, Georgia, developed the technology to deodorize cottonseed oil, creating the very first edible vegetable oil known in the industry. In 1900, Wesson started a refinery in Savannah to produce Wesson oil for the retail market. Wesson later developed the hydrogenation process used to produce a "hogless lard" called Snowdrift, laying the foundation for the highly successful Wesson Oil & Snowdrift Company.

In 1960, the company merged with Hunt Foods & Industries, founded as the Hunt Brothers Fruit Packaging Company in 1890 by Joseph and William Hancock Hunt in Santa Rosa, California, to become Hunt-Wesson, Inc. The company was acquired in 1990 by ConAgra, Inc., founded in 1919 when four flour mills joined to form Nebraska Consolidated Mills, headquartered in Omaha.

Ingredient
Corn oil

Strange Facts
■ Corn oil is obtained from the germ of the kernel. The crude oil is extracted by crushing and milling the kernels. Caustic soda is mixed into the oil and heated, allowing most of the impurities and fatty acids to separate from the oil. Bleaching clay is then added under vacuum at elevated temperatures to remove the color from the oil. The oil is then placed in a vacuum, and steam is forced though it, deodorizing the refined oil. The result is a pure, delicate oil with a natural flavor and taste.

■ Today all Wesson oil available to the public is packaged in plastic bottles. The last glass bottle was used in 1984.

■ Florence Henderson, best known as Carol Brady on *The Brady Bunch*, was spokesperson for Wesson oil for many years on television, touting "Wessonality."

Distribution
■ Wesson was the first vegetable oil on the market.

■ Wesson makes Wesson All Natural Vegetable Oil (from soybean oil), Wesson Corn Oil, Wesson Sunflower Oil, Wesson Canola Oil, Wesson Best Blend, Wesson Stir Fry Oil, Wesson No-Stick Cooking Spray, and Wesson Shortening.

For More Information

Hunt-Wesson, Inc., P.O. Box 4800, Fullerton, CA 92633. Or telephone 1-714-680-1000.

Spearmint Gum

■ **Lure crabs.** Chew a piece of Wrigley's Spearmint Gum briefly and use it as bait on a fishing line.

■ **Repair a leaking gas tank temporarily.** Patch the leak with a piece of well-chewed Wrigley's Spearmint Gum.

■ **Alleviate an earache caused by a cold, sinus infection, or allergy.** The muscular action of chewing Wrigley's Spearmint Gum will open the eustachian tubes (leading from the back of the throat to the middle ear).

■ **Seal a punctured garden hose.** Patch the holes with chewed Wrigley's Spearmint Gum.

■ **Keep mealworms and other pests away from pasta.** Place a few sticks of wrapped Wrigley's Spearmint Gum on the shelf near open packages of noodles, macaroni, or spaghetti. Spearmint repels these household pests.

■ **Adhere plastic bathroom tiles.** If a tile comes loose, put a little piece of chewed Wrigley's Spearmint Gum on each corner and press back in place.

■ **Fill cracks in a wall or in a clay flowerpot.** Use a well-chewed stick of Wrigley's Spearmint Gum.

■ **Relieve an earache caused by the change in pressure in an airplane.** Open the eustachian tubes in your ears by chewing Wrigley's Spearmint Gum on an airplane flight.

■ **Repair a loose pane of glass temporarily.** Use a wad of chewed Wrigley's Spearmint Gum as window putty.

■ **Fix eyeglasses.** In an emergency, put a small piece of chewed Wrigley's Spearmint Gum in the corner of the lens to hold it in place.

■ **Improvise caulking compound.** Use a piece of well-chewed Wrigley's Spearmint Gum to seal holes.

■ **Fix a hem temporarily.** Reattach a drooping hem with a dab of chewed Wrigley's Spearmint Gum.

■ **Retrieve a coin or piece of jewelry that has fallen down a drain.** Tie a fishing weight to a long string, chew a piece of Wrigley's Spearmint Gum briefly, stick it on the bottom of the weight, dangle it down the drain, let it take hold, then pull up.

Invented
1893

The Name

Wrigley's Spearmint Gum is named after company founder William Wrigley Jr. and the common garden mint (*Mentha spicata*), better known as spearmint because of the sharp point of its leaves.

A Short History

William Wrigley Jr. started his career at the age of thirteen when, following his expulsion from school, his father put him to work selling soap door-to-door. In 1891 he moved to Chicago to sell soap and baking powder. At twenty-nine, he started his own business in Chicago—with a wife and child and $32 in cash. When he began offering customers free chewing gum made of spruce gum and paraffin by Zeno Manufacturing, customers offered to buy the gum. Convinced that chicle, a naturally sweet gum base being imported from Central America for the rubber industry, would work as a main ingredient in chewing gum, Wrigley developed two gum flavors, Lotta Gum and Vassar. In 1893, Wrigley introduced Spearmint and Juicy Fruit gums, offering dealers counter scales, cash registers, and display cases for volume purchases. In 1898, he merged with Zeno Manufacturing to form Wm. Wrigley Jr. & Co, and by 1910, after pumping huge amounts of money into advertising, Wrigley's Spearmint Gum was the leading U.S. brand.

Ingredients

Sugar, gum base, corn syrup, dextrose, softeners, natural flavors and BHT (to maintain freshness)

Strange Facts

■ In 1915, William Wrigley Jr. sent four free sticks of gum to every person listed in a U.S. phone book.

■ The spear-bodied elf character William Wrigley began using before World War I to promote Wrigley's Spearmint Gum turned into the cheerful Wrigley gum boy of the 1960s.

■ During World War II, gum, considered an emergency ration, was also given to soldiers to relieve tension and dry throats on long marches. GIs used chewed gum to patch jeep tires, gas tanks, life rafts, and parts of airplanes. Wrigley advertisements recommended five sticks of gum per day for every war worker, insisting that "Factory tests show how chewing gum helps men feel better, work better."

■ William Wrigley was the first distributor to place gum next to restaurant cash registers.

■ The Wrigley family bought Catalina Island in 1919 and the Arizona Biltmore Hotel in 1931, built the Wrigley building in Chicago in 1924, and owned the Chicago Cubs for fifty-seven years.

■ The company did not raise the original five-cent price of Spearmint, Juicy Fruit, and Doublemint gums until 1971, when management reluctantly agreed to raise it to seven cents.

■ Before World War II, the basic ingredient of all chewing gum was chicle, the sap of the sapodilla tree indigenous to Central and South America. When chicle became difficult to obtain during World War II, the gum industry developed synthetic gum bases such as polyvinyl acetate, supplied almost entirely by the Hercule Powder Company, an explosives manufacturer.

■ Psychiatrists have called gum chewing oral masturbation.

■ Americans chew approximately $2.5 billion worth of gum every year.

■ The average American chews 168 sticks of gum each year.

■ According to *The Great American Chewing Gum Book* by Robert Hendrickson, if all the sticks of gum chewed in America each year were laid end to end, it would equal a stick of gum five million miles long. That's long enough to reach the moon and back ten times.

■ Since World War II, American soldiers have been issued gum with their K rations and survival kits.

■ William Wrigley Jr.'s grandson, William Wrigley, owns 25 percent of the company and serves as CEO.

Distribution

■ In 1993, the Wm. Wrigley Jr. Company sold over $1.4 billion worth of gum.

■ The Wm. Wrigley Jr. Company has 49 percent of the $1.6 billion domestic gum market and is the number-one chewing gum maker in the world.

■ Since the collapse of communism, Wrigley's sales to the former Soviet Union have surged about 20 percent every year since 1989. For two years in a row, sales of Juicy Fruit, Hubba Bubba, Big Boy, and other Wrigley's brands doubled in Central and Eastern Europe. Foreign sales now account for 45 percent of the company's business.

■ Wrigley gums include Arrowmint, Big Boy, Big G, Big

Red, Cool Crunch, Doublemint, Dulce 16, Extra, Freedent, Hubba Bubba, Juicy Fruit, Orbit, P.K., Spearmint, and Winterfresh.

For More Information

Wm. Wrigley Jr. Company, 410 North Michigan Avenue, Chicago, IL 60611. Or telephone 1-312-644-2121.

And Much, Much More

Heinz® Ketchup®

Clean tarnish from copper. Rub with Ketchup. **For More Information:** H. J. Heinz Co., P.O. Box 57, Pittsburgh, PA 15230. Or telephone 1-412-456-5700.

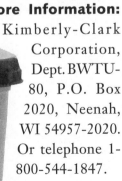

Huggies® Baby Wipes

Blot up spilled coffee from a rug or carpet. Huggies Baby Wipes absorb coffee without leaving a large stain. **For More Information:** Kimberly-Clark Corporation, Dept. BWTU-80, P.O. Box 2020, Neenah, WI 54957-2020. Or telephone 1-800-544-1847.

Parsons'® Ammonia

Clean jewelry. Soak in equal parts of Parsons' Ammonia and warm water for ten minutes. Rub gently with a cloth or soft brush and allow to air dry. Do not use on pearls. **For More Information:** The Dial Corporation, Consumer Information Center, 15101 N. Scottsdale Road, Scottsdale, AZ 85254. Or telephone 1-800-528-0849.

Scotchgard®

Make ski pants. Spray a pair of old jeans with Scotchgard. Be sure to wear long underwear for warmth. **For More Information:** 3M Home & Commercial Care Products, P.O. Box 33068, St. Paul, MN 55133. Or telephone 1-800-364-3577.

If you know more offbeat uses for brand-name products, send your tips and suggestions to:
Joey Green
Paint Your House with Powdered Milk
c/o Hyperion
114 Fifth Avenue
New York, NY 10011

Acknowledgments

Once again my editor, Laurie Abkemeier, made working on this book a pure joy. I am grateful for her finesse, passion, sharp wit, and love for pop culture.

I am also indebted to the outstanding talents of Samantha Miller, Claudyne Bedell, Bob Miller, Adrian James, Jeremy Solomon, Kim from L.A., Bob Baskinsherry, and a battalion of copyeditors and proofreaders.

In the corporate world, I take my hat off to Gary Lyons at Cadbury Beverages Inc. (makers of Canada Dry Club Soda), Rita Henderson and Carol Takata at Nestlé (makers of Carnation Nonfat Dry Milk), Sandy Sullivan at The Clorox Company (makers of Clorox and S.O.S), Nancy Ganassini and Tom Soli at Conair Corporation (makers of the Conair Pro Style 1600), Charles Oppenheimer at Schering-Plough HealthCare Products, Inc. (makers of Coppertone sunscreen), Sylvia Woolf Gallop at Binney & Smith Inc. (makers of Crayola Chalk and Crayola Crayons), Diane J. Hamel and Genelle Watts-Jackson at McCormick & Company, Inc. (makers of McCormick/Schilling Cream of Tartar, Food Coloring, and Vanilla Extract), Thomas Rowland at First Brands Corporation (makers of GLAD Trash Bags), Pam Becker at General Mills (makers of Gold Medal Flour), Mitchell A. Frank at Best Foods, CPC International Inc. (makers of Kingsford's Corn Starch), Lawrence Hicks at Thomas J. Lipton Company (makers of Lipton Tea Bags), John N. O'Shea at Warner-Lambert Company (makers of

Lubriderm), Nancy Maffucci at MasterCard International, Sharon Ptak Miles at Kraft Foods, Inc. (makers of Maxwell House Coffee), James Koester at Miller Brewing Company (makers of Miller High Life), Ellen Ciuzio at American Home Foods, Inc. (makers of Pam No Stick Cooking Spray), Alan McDonald, Pat Schweitzer, Tom Krusinis, and Joe Vagi at Reynolds Metals Company (makers of Reynolds Cut-Rite Wax Paper), Alan Rames and Judy Schuster at 3M (makers of Scotch Transparent Tape and Scotchgard), Joseph J. Bonk at DowBrands (makers of Spray 'n Wash), Gary Evans at Sioux Honey Association (makers of SueBee Honey), Paul McIlhenny at McIlhenny Company (makers of Tabasco pepper sauce), Charles A. Tornabene at Turtle Wax, Inc., Kurt Ganderup at U.S. Borax, Inc. (owners of the 20 Mule Team trademark), Nancy Lee Carter at Kimberly-Clark Corporation (makers of VIVA Ultra paper towels), Karen Johnston at Hunt Wesson, Inc. (makers of Wesson Corn Oil), Anne Marie Vela at the Wm. Wrigley Jr. Company (makers of Wrigley's Spearmint Gum), Deborah Magness and Scott Thayer at Heinz U.S.A. (makers of Heinz Ketchup), Robert G. Evans at Kimberly-Clark Corporation (makers of Huggies Baby Wipes), and John Burton at The Dial Corp. (makers of Parsons' Ammonia).

Upstanding Americans who shared their ingenuity include Robert and Barbara Green, Lora and Barry Schwartzberg, Cindy Press, John Fiorre Pucci, Howard Gerhsen, Robin and Amy Robinson, Robin Rouda, Bill Aitchison, and Kathy McMahon.

Above all, all my love to Debbie, Ashley, and Julia.

The Fine Print

Sources

■ *All-New Hints from Heloise* by Heloise (New York: Perigee, 1989)

■ *Another Use For* by Vicki Lansky (Deephaven, MN: Book Peddlers, 1991)

■ *Ask Anne & Nan* by Anne Adams and Nancy Walker (Brattleboro, VT: Whetstone, 1989)

■ *Can You Trust a Tomato in January?* by Vince Staten (New York: Simon & Schuster, 1993)

■ *Dictionary of Trade Name Origins* by Adrian Room (London: Routledge & Kegan Paul, 1982)

■ *The Doctors Book of Home Remedies* by the Editors of Prevention Magazine (Emmaus, PA: Rodale Press, 1990)

■ *Encyclopedia of Pop Culture* by Jane & Michael Stern (New York: HarperCollins, 1992)

■ *Famous American Trademarks* by Arnold B. Barach (Washington, D.C.: Public Affairs Press, 1971).

■ *From Beer to Eternity* by Will Anderson (Lexington, MA: The Stephen Greene Press, 1987)

■ *Hints from Heloise* by Heloise (New York: Arbor House, 1980)

■ *Hoover's Handbook of World Business 1993* (Austin: Reference Press, 1993)

■ *Hoover's Handbook of American Business 1994* (Austin: Reference Press, 1994)

■ *Household Hints & Handy Tips* by Reader's Digest (Pleasantville, NY: Reader's Digest Association, 1988)

■ *How the Cadillac Got Its Fins* by Jack Mingo (New York: HarperCollins, 1994)

■ *I'll Buy That!* by the Editors of Consumer Reports (Mount Vernon, NY: Consumers Union, 1986)

■ *Kitchen Medicines* by Ben Charles Harris (Barre, MA: Barre, 1968)

■ *Make It Yourself* by Dolores Riccio and Joan Bingham (Radnor, PA: Chilton, 1978)

■ *Mary Ellen's Best of Helpful Hints* by Mary Ellen Pinkham (New York: Warner/B. Lansky, 1979)

■ *Mary Ellen's Greatest Hints* by Mary Ellen Pinkham (New York: Fawcett Crest, 1990)

■ *Our Story So Far* (St. Paul, MN: 3M, 1977)

■ *Panati's Extraordinary Origins of Everyday Things* by Charles Panati (New York: HarperCollins, 1987)

■ *Practical Problem Solver* by Reader's Digest (Pleasantville, NY: Reader's Digest, 1991)

■ *Rodale's Book of Hints, Tips & Everyday Wisdom* by Carol Hupping, Cheryl Winters Tetreau, and Roger B. Yepsen, Jr. (Emmaus, PA: Rodale Press, 1985)

■ *Symbols of America* by Hal Morgan (New York: Viking, 1986)

■ *The Tabasco Cookbook* by Paul McIlhenny with Barbara Hunter (New York: Clarkson Potter, 1993)

■ *Why Did They Name It . . . ?* by Hannah Campbell (New York: Fleet, 1964)

■ *The Woman's Day Help Book* by Geraldine Rhoads and Edna Paradis (New York: Viking, 1988)

Trademark Information

"Canada Dry", and the shield are registered trademarks of Cadbury Beverages Inc.

"Carnation" is a registered trademark of Nestlé Food Company.

"Clorox" is a registered trademark of The Clorox Company.

"Conair" and "Pro Style" are registered trademarks of Conair Corporation.

"Coppertone" is a registered trademark of Schering-Plough HealthCare Products, Inc. Photograph reproduced with permission of Schering-Plough HealthCare Products, Inc., the copyright owner.

"Crayola" is a registered trademark of Binney & Smith Inc.

"McCormick" and "Schilling" are registered trademarks of McCormick & Co. Inc.

"GLAD" is a registered trademark of First Brands Corporation.

"Gold Medal" is a registered trademark of General Mills, Inc.

"Kingsford's" and the Kingsford logo are registered trademarks of CPC International Inc.

"Lipton," "The 'Brisk' Tea," and "Flo-Thru" are registered trademarks of Thomas J. Lipton Company.

"Lubriderm" is a registered trademark of Warner-Lambert Co.

"MasterCard" is a registered trademark of MasterCard International.

"Maxwell House" and "Good to the Last Drop" are registered trademarks of Kraft Foods, Inc. Photograph used with permission.

"Miller" and "High Life" are registered trademarks of the Miller Brewing Company.

"Pam No Stick Cooking Spray" is a registered trademark of American Home Food Products, Inc.

"Reynolds" and "Cut-Rite" are registered trademarks of Reynolds Metals Company.

"Scotch," "3M," and the plaid design are registered trademarks of 3M.

"S.O.S" is a registered trademark of The Clorox Company.

"Spray 'n Wash" is a registered trademark of DowBrands L.P.

"SueBee" is a registered trademark of Sioux Honey Association.

Index

Corn, de-silking
VIVA Ultra paper towels, 141
Coughs, relieving
SueBee Honey, 110
Countertops, cleaning
Canada Dry Club Soda, 2
Crabs, luring
Wrigley's Spearmint Gum, 151
Crayon
carrier, Clorox bleach, 12
remover, Conair Pro Style 1600,
17; S.O.S Steel Wool Soap Pads,
103; VIVA Ultra paper towels,
140
Cutting boards
Wesson Corn Oil, 146

Dampness, preventing
Crayola Chalk, 28
Decals, removing
Wesson Corn Oil, 146
Deodorizers
air, Lipton Tea Bags, 62
carpet, 20 Mule Team Borax, 129,
130
clothes, 20 Mule Team Borax, 130
coolers, Clorox bleach, 10
freezer, Maxwell House Coffee, 76
garbage cans, Clorox bleach, 10
garbage disposal, Clorox bleach, 14
paint, Vanilla Extract, 136
refrigerator, Maxwell House Coffee, 76
thermos bottles, Clorox bleach, 10
Diamonds, cleaning
Canada Dry Club Soda, 1
Diaper
changing pad, Reynolds Cut-Rite
Wax Paper, 93

deodorizing, 20 Mule Team Borax,
130
Diarrhea, relieving
Lipton Tea Bags, 62
Dishwasher runners
Pam No Stick Cooking Spray, 88
Dogs
burrs and tar, Wesson Corn Oil,
147
clogged drains, S.O.S Steel Wool
Soap Pads, 104
coat, Wesson Corn Oil, 145
dry shampoo, Kingsford's Corn
Starch, 57
Doors
locked, MasterCard, 70
squeaky, Pam No Stick Cooking
Spray, 88
Dough
Pam No Stick Cooking Spray, 89
Drains
S.O.S Steel Wool Soap Pads, 104
Dried glue, removing
Coppertone, 24
Dry shampoo
Kingsford's Corn Starch, 56
Dry skin
Lubriderm, 67
Dumbbells
Clorox bleach, 14
Dust
Conair Pro Style 1600, 18
GLAD Trash Bags, 47
Turtle Wax, 124

Earache
Wrigley's Spearmint Gum, 151
Eggs, differentiating
Crayola Crayons, 32

Food Coloring, 41
Electric beater
Reynolds Cut-Rite Wax Paper, 92
Electrical outlets, covering
Scotch Transparent Tape, 99
Emeralds, cleaning
Canada Dry Club Soda, 1
Emergency lights
Maxwell House Coffee, 76
Envelopes, sealing
Crayola Crayons, 32
Erysipelas, relieving
SueBee Honey, 111
Eyeglasses, repairing
Scotch Transparent Tape, 98
Wrigley's Spearmint Gum, 152
Eyes, soothing
Lipton Tea Bags, 62

Fabric dye
Lipton Tea Bags, 61
Maxwell House Coffee, 74
Facial
SueBee Honey, 109
Feet
deodorizing, Lipton Tea Bags, 61
soothing, Wesson Corn Oil, 147
Fertilizer
Miller High Life, 80
Maxwell House Coffee, 74, 75
Fingernails
Coppertone, 23
Lipton Tea Bags, 63
MasterCard, 70
Fingerpaints
Food Coloring, 41
Kingsford's Corn Starch, 57
First aid
SueBee Honey, 109

Fish
bait, Maxwell House Coffee, 75
defrosting, Carnation, 6
tank water, Food Coloring, 41
Flame retardant
20 Mule Team Borax, 128
Floors
Reynolds Cut-Rite Wax Paper, 94
Flowers
arranging, Scotch Transparent Tape, 97
preserving, 20 Mule Team Borax, 127
prolonging, Clorox bleach, 10
tinting, Food Coloring, 41
Formica, scratches
Crayola Crayons, 31
Freezer
defrosting, Pam No Stick Cooking Spray, 88
deodorizing, Maxwell House Coffee, 76
Fruits, harvesting
Clorox bleach, 13
Funnel, improvising
Clorox bleach, 13
Furniture
drawers, lubricating, Turtle Wax, 123
polishing, Coppertone, 23; Turtle Wax, 123
removing excess polish, Kingsford's Corn Starch, 57
removing glue, Wesson Corn Oil, 147
scratches, Crayola Crayons, 31

Garbage
cans, Clorox bleach, 10

Nail caddie
Scotch Transparent Tape, 98
Nail polish, drying
Pam No Stick Cooking Spray, 87
Necklace, restringing
Scotch Transparent Tape, 98
Newspaper clippings, preserving
Canada Dry Club Soda, 3

Outdoor cushions, stuffing
GLAD Trash Bags, 47
Outdoor siding
Clorox bleach, 10

Paint
bucket, Clorox bleach, 13
chandeliers, GLAD Trash Bags, 46
cleaning, Coppertone, 23
deodorizer, Vanilla Extract, 136
remover, Wesson Corn Oil, 146
scraping, MasterCard, 70
storing, Reynolds Cut-Rite Wax
Paper, 94
substitute, Carnation, 8
Paintbrushes, storing
Maxwell House Coffee, 75
Pancakes
Canada Dry Club Soda, 1
Panty hose
drying, Conair Pro Style 1600, 18
snag, Scotch Transparent Tape, 98
Papier-mâché
Gold Medal flour, 51
Pastry dough, sticky
Kingsford's Corn Starch, 57
Patios
Clorox bleach, 10

Pincushion
S.O.S Steel Wool Soap Pads, 103
Pipe joints, lubricating
Coppertone, 24
Pipes, defrosting frozen
Conair Pro Style 1600, 18
Plants
Canada Dry Club Soda, 2
Carnation, 7
Plastic sheet
GLAD Trash Bags, 48
Plastic tablecloths, removing
wrinkles
Conair Pro Style 1600, 19
Plate, cracked
Carnation, 7
Play Dough
Gold Medal flour, 51
Playing cards, cleaning
Gold Medal flour, 52
Kingsford's Corn Starch, 57
Turtle Wax, 124
Poison ivy
Carnation, 6
Pooper scooper
Clorox bleach, 11
Popcorn
Pam No Stick Cooking Spray, 88
Tabasco pepper sauce, 117
Porcelain
Canada Dry Club Soda, 2
Clorox bleach, 12
Cream of Tartar, 38
20 Mule Team Borax, 129
Prescription labels
Scotch Transparent Tape, 98
Price tag, removing
Wesson Corn Oil, 147

About the Author

Joey Green, author of *Polish Your Furniture with Panty Hose*, got Jay Leno to shave with Jif peanut butter on *The Tonight Show*, had Katie Couric drop her diamond engagement ring in a glass of Efferdent on *The Today Show*, and has been seen polishing furniture with SPAM on *CNN Headline News* and cleaning a toilet with Coca-Cola in *The New York Times*. A former contributing editor to *National Lampoon* and a former advertising copywriter at J. Walter Thompson, Green is the author of several books, including *Selling Out: If Famous Authors Wrote Advertising, Hi Bob! (A Self-Help Guide to the Bob Newhart Show)*, and *The Partridge Family Album*. A native of Miami, Florida, and a graduate of Cornell University, he wrote television commercials for Burger King and Walt Disney World, and won a Clio Award for a print ad he created for Eastman Kodak. He backpacked around the world for two years on his honeymoon, and currently lives in Los Angeles with his wife, Debbie, and their two daughters, Ashley and Julia.

Get the Book That Started the Craze!